Inspired

TO THE CROSS

JON KENNEDY

First printing

Some names and identifying details may have been changed to protect the privacy of individuals.

ISBN: 979-8-218-30067-8

Book design by Saqib Arshad

For I know the plans I have for you, declares the Lord, plans to prosper you and not to harm you, plans to give you a hope and a future.

JEREMIAH 29:11

****

Then you will call on me and come and pray to me, and I will listen to you. You will seek me and find me when you seek me with ALL your heart.

JEREMIAH 29:12-13

This book is dedicated to my wife, Kim and my children and grandchildren.

Who would have ever thought when we met in sixth grade in 1985 that 38 years later, we would be married with three beautiful children we are so proud of, and then blessed with three beautiful grandchildren? Our journey hasn't been easy at times and our hands are weathered and scarred from the trials and storms of life, but we are still together. They say every marriage comes to points when love becomes a choice. I am so glad in the deep valleys we chose love. Love conquers all! When you get out of the valley it makes the view and pleasure of the mountains more breathtaking and glamorous. I believe that anytime I have seen a man being used by God there is an incredibly strong woman by his side. You are that woman.

The most important message of this book is that those who do not know Jesus come to know Him as their Lord and Savior, that those backslidden would recommit to Him, and those walking with God would go deeper. I also hope that those who read about our marriage realize it's not perfect, but we are committed and have learned to become good forgivers of each other.

I ask God to help me to love and cherish you and make you realize and feel how special you are to me, till death do us part. The best is yet to come!

Devyn, JonMichael and Jillian, I am so proud of each of you beyond words. What I admire most about each of you is your kind, compassionate, loving hearts. Devyn and JonMichael, you have children of your own and can understand the love a parent has for their children. Jillian will one day too understand. I love all of you and my love is unconditional. There is nothing you could ever do to stop that love. Although you were baptized as babies, I have had a vision of baptizing each of you as adults who made the choice to serve God on your own. I pray that this vision will one day come to fruition like this book has, and that God continues to help me to be the best father I can humanly be to each of you.

Camille, Mila, and Grayson, you are too young to read this, but I pray that I am the most loving, patient, and gentle Papa. I want you to always know how special you are to Grammy and I and want you to always remember how much we love you!

Reviews

Jon Kennedy's life is a tapestry of high highs and low lows. *Inspired to the Cross*, shares the saga of a childhood filled with disappointment and loss, temptation, and trial. The family he loved so deeply, like most families, was sifted and tried. From the tragic loss of his older brother, Jimmy, in a work accident, to the rebellion of his older sister, Shannon, to the drug addiction of his sister, Laurel, to the frustrations of daily life, Jon tells his story in all its brutal honesty.

And yet, through the amazing grace of God, Jon's story is also one of redemption! God broke through the tragedy and brought triumph. No, every cloud doesn't have a silver lining. But Jon's story is the testimony of God's faithfulness even through the deepest valleys and the darkest days. Through the pain and struggle, God has brought hope and healing and salvation.

If you want a good dose of truth, *Inspired to the Cross* will bring it. Jon's heart shines through each page. And even more importantly, Jesus Christ is honored for who He is: the Way, the Truth, and the Life.

— *Dr. Rex Keener, Senior and Founding Pastor of*
Grace Fellowship Church

****

What a powerful testimony of God at work through Jon Kennedy! Jon's vulnerability in sharing his own struggles (and by God's grace, his triumphs) are a true inspiration and encouragement to boldly share our own testimonies. Jon's writing style engages readers by encouraging and challenging them—then assuring them of God's all-encompassing love and grace. This book will bless many!

—*Tom Roemke, Former Principal, Our Savior's School*

****

Straight from the heart. No matter where you are in your walk of life, the message is: compassion, repentance, faith, grace, discernment, and self-evaluation, all of which are needed in this world. Inspiration can come from different sources, and this is one of them. Well done!

— *Michael Kenny*

****

Inspired to the Cross is an outstanding, must-read book! An amazing human interest story that truly inspires building a relationship with God, fills you with hope, and renews your faith. No other book has ever reached my heart and soul from start to finish as this one has. My hope is that everyone I love and as many people as possible are blessed enough to read it. It will change their lives because it's based on faith, love, and truth throughout!

— *Nancy Giffen*

****

Impressed by the way Jon explains his journey. He keeps it "real." Very inspirational and moving. Definitely an encouraging book!

— *Daniel Valenti, Author*

****

Jon's journey is inspirational, and his openness about real-life, personal situations is very relatable. The correlations to Biblical texts offer hope and direction to those struggling through their own issues. Jon's writing style engages the reader to refer to the Bible for further understanding. This story depicts God's love, presence, and His forgiveness.

— *Nicholas J. Audi*

****

The Christ-centered autobiography of Jon Kennedy is a gift to all of us who long to see the extraordinary love and hope of God through the ordinary and the chaos. Jon has drawn us into his stories and testimonies about God, with such a relational and unassuming manner. He is blessed with a consistent hunger and thirst for righteousness in Christ, the antithesis of spiritual sloth, and an excellent example for us fellow believers.

— *Dr. B*

****

I thoroughly enjoyed reading *Inspired to the Cross*. Jon Kennedy is a friend and inspiration to my own challenging walk. His book shares real-life accounts that relate so much to events and struggles we all encounter and share. Jon shares his own journey while using Scripture from the Bible to reveal its true meaning. I highly recommend this book to all, no matter where they are in their Christian journey!

— *John Audi*

****

Inspired to the Cross is a very inspiring and powerful read! Written by someone who has personally experienced the presence of God in his life, as is evident by his numerous stories and divine appointments. Most encouraging and uplifting! I would recommend this book to those who already have a relationship with Christ to assist them in their daily walk, and to those who are still searching. God is working!

— *Warren C. DeLollo, Pastor of Missions*

****

The true story of a man's life experiences (the good and the tragic). He becomes a humbled man who realizes the only escape from darkness into light is to put "God First in Everything." A truly inspirational story!

— *Jed Giffen*

****

I know and believe Jon's writing was a gift from God, as well as his speaking ability. Jon had neither of these as a child. God heard my prayer when I dedicated him from my womb. May this book encourage all who need to know that God sees them and wants a relationship with them. He has a plan for each of our lives. One of God's names is El Roi, pronounced El-Raw-ee, which means, "The God who knows me." Blessings and encouragement to all who read this book.

— *Thelma Kennedy (Jon's mother)*

Foreword

My friend, Jon Kennedy wrote this special book, *Inspired to The Cross*, which consists of his own personal experiences and reflections of his life journey. Jon is a man of many unique talents, who shares his faith and gifts with others in subtle ways.

I have known Jon for 25 years. We met when he did a landscaping job at our house. His work is done with great care, and attention to detail. Our friendship grew from there, and we shared many conversations about faith and the trials and tribulations of life.

Jon's genuine kindness toward our dear mother during her struggles with dementia was such an inspiration to me. I knew there was something very special about this friend, who took the time to pray with our mom at home. He also visited Mom at the nursing home, once her condition worsened. He was a constant source of support and faith. I felt honored to have such a caring, faith-filled friend.

Jon shares a faithful, loving relationship with his beautiful family. I've had the pleasure of being at their home for various occasions, and I could see firsthand that they make God the center of their family unit.

I know you will enjoy reading Jon's book, and you will also be Inspired to the Cross!

—*Nicholas J. Audi (Retired School Principal)*

Preface

For so long, I would leave the presence of such broken people and say to myself, "I wish I had a book of my life to share with them. To show them there's a God who loves them, who will walk with them, and is faithful."

Never in my wildest dreams did I think I would write a book. I didn't even know I had the ability to write. Then God takes a thought and makes it a dream, a vision, and brings it to fruition with the most unlikely person. Without exaggeration, I did not read one book till I was in my late thirties...not one! I thought to myself, *Lord, you have the wrong guy!* Our amazing, loving God has a sense of humor.

Through this journey I will share what the Lord allowed me to see one day in the spiritual realm—the realm the human eye can't see.

(Ephesians 6:12): *"For we wrestle not against flesh and blood, but against principalities, against powers, against the rulers of the darkness of this world, against spiritual wickedness in high places."*

If you don't think you are in a spiritual battle, you have already lost the war. I will share what I heard one special day from God that completely validates one of the most important verses in the Bible:

(John 3:16): *"For God so loved the world, that He gave His only begotten son, that whosoever believeth in Him should not perish, but have everlasting life."*

As we journey together, you will grasp that it is a gift to know God and it is something to be treasured. When you look at the sun, moon, stars, the beach, mountains, when you hold that precious infant for the first time, you know personally its Creator. You can know the Creator of all things! It is your choice.

There are many promises in the Bible from a faithful God, but they are only for those who love and fear the Lord. They are not for everyone. His love letter—the Bible—from your Creator, will make you the best father, mother, brother, sister, friend, employee, or business owner you can be. It is your blueprint for life; it holds the keys to love, peace, and happiness. It is not absent of pain and suffering, but you have a God who will walk through everything with you and never leave or forsake you (Hebrews 13:5). He will give you a peace beyond understanding in any storm you face (Philippians 4:7). We not only have the gift of eternity with Him, absent of pain and suffering, and united with other loved ones who were also in Christ Jesus, but also the benefit of getting to know Him as He helps us navigate life and shows us how much He loves us. We are intimately known by Him. Remember, God created us to commune with Him, to have a relationship with Him. We are His pleasure.

My heart breaks in today's society with the recent pandemic, food shortages, the cost of living becoming unbearable, crime and our safety and security under attack, rumors of nuclear war, and incredible instability. Anxiety, depression, and suicide are on a steady rise. Life is hard at times. So many people are walking this journey called life alone without their Creator. Many are so broken and fighting to keep it together, filled with fear, panic, and despair. Some are sick and fighting for their lives from diseases that riddle their bodies. Whatever the person, situation, circumstance, or sickness may be, there is a God of the impossible with His hand held out. If they would only put their hand in His, there is peace in the storm, a safety net knowing God is with you.

I pray I can alleviate some misconceptions you might have about Christians. A true Christian represents Jesus. They should be loving, humble, kind, compassionate, generous, and joyful. They are not perfect; no one is. We are to look to Jesus, not to Christians. He is our guide. Christians are never to judge, ever. I heard in a sermon that Anne Graham Lotz preached, that was about a conversation with her dad, Billy Graham, he said, "It's our job to love, the Holy Spirit's job to convict, and God's job to judge." We can have the gift of prophecy, of healing, but without love we have *nothing*!

I believe with all my heart that the Bible is completely true and infallible. It is a miracle from God to us. My two major experiences with my eyes and ears validate that. What kind of person would I be if I didn't warn you that you're on the edge of an abyss about to fall over? I will not take one dime from any royalties from this book, to show there are no ulterior motives to my writing. I love helping broken people to get back to solid ground. I was once in their shoes and wouldn't be where I am today without God. I enjoy witnessing the love that so many of my friends and family have for each other and want them to protect that love forever. I want everyone to not only experience and reap the benefits of knowing and walking with God, but to have peace in these turbulent days and in the good times and bad, with absolute certainty that your hand is in the Creator's and no matter what, He is with you.

My life is not perfect, and my family is not perfect. We have our struggles. I hope those who read this book don't get the impression that I think I am "holier than thou." I have to fight sin in my life and guard my heart daily. We all sin and fall short of the glory of God (Romans 3:23). I am just your average, ordinary guy who loves God. I am a sinner with a past, just like everyone else, but like the Apostle

Paul said, "Put your past behind you and strive for the goal." It's not my job to judge anyone, it's my job to love, but yes, there are those who I must get on my knees and ask God for help to love. I am human, after all.

In reading this book, I hope that you will grasp what I have seen and heard. **I share the biggest mistake of my life and because of that mistake it caused many, many more mistakes.** I share twists and turns, detours, and many amazing stories of God's incredible love and faithfulness throughout my life.

I hope you will take this journey with me and begin to see why I whole-heartedly believe in the One to which I pray and write about.

They say what comes from the heart reaches the heart, and that is my prayer. I know not everyone goes to Heaven but those that know and make Jesus Lord and Savior of their lives will. So, I ask this question: Do you love your children, your spouse, your parents, your friends? Don't you want to be with them forever, without end, in the presence of our Holy, loving God?

Come on this journey with me, I pray that every word touches your heart and you become Inspired to the Cross!

Contents

The Beginning of the Journey

What is the earliest memory you have from your childhood? I've heard some people say they remember being in their crib. Someone even told me they remember coming through the birth canal.

My first memory was when I was four or five years old and I was on the living room floor playing with some toys. It was a beautiful day, the sun was beaming through the picture window, and I could feel the warmth, but more importantly, I felt loved and content.

I was the youngest of five children. I remember the whole family around the dinner table, and we would begin by saying Grace and giving thanks to God. Sometimes my older sister and I would get into trouble from giggling about something during prayer.

I remember all of us sitting as a family on Christmas taking turns opening presents. Back then we got one nice thing and the other few gifts were necessities like socks and gloves. The gifts weren't as important as the love and contentment that I felt. As the years went on, things took a turn for the worst. I think it was my grandmother's passing from cancer in 1979 that really started the downward spiral for our family. I was six years old.

Being the youngest child in a large family, and due to circumstances beyond my parents' control, I was exposed to so many things that a child shouldn't be exposed to. My parents both had to work during the day and many times had side businesses which consumed many nights. When I was younger they would get us a babysitter when they weren't home, but as my sister Laurel and I got a little older, our older siblings would keep an eye on us. Our house became a neighborhood hangout when my parents weren't around because of work. We literally had a neighborhood full of kids who were the same age as my older siblings. They were all good, normal teenagers, just doing things they were not supposed to be doing. At that time the drinking age was eighteen. I remember all the kids drinking, smoking cigarettes, and smoking pot. My oldest sister would give me hits off the joint and watch me "bounce off the walls". I was between eight and ten years old when she did this.

****

I was way ahead of myself for my age because I was constantly around my older siblings and their friends, which years later would provide an easy transition to things I shouldn't have been doing. Most kids were playing with toys and I was getting hits off joints. Even so, as I look back on my childhood, I feel I enjoyed it; sure, there are many things I would have changed but I loved my siblings and I loved my parents.

My parents did the best they could to raise our family. They taught us right from wrong and my dad ingrained in us respect and manners, but sometimes the baggage we carry from childhood and our upbringing affects us more than we know. My mother was raised in a traditional home and went to church weekly. We were a traditional family but we weren't perfect. My mom would drag all five of us to church and we would give her such a hard time. Even as a six-year-old child I would think to myself, *why does she bother?* I understand now the importance of getting us to church and appreciate that she didn't give up. My father at this point did not go to church or help my mom in the process, so the house at that point was spiritually divided.

My dad (which I will share in more detail later) was either stolen or illegally adopted. He never knew his biological parents and had no way of finding them. The woman he called "Mom" was not very loving. My dad believes she orchestrated their relationship so that one day he could take care of her. The man he called "Dad" was an alcoholic.

Church was nonexistent for my dad when he was growing up, but he did say at twelve years old he would walk to the local church occasionally, sit in the back, and throw a few cents into the offering basket. I believe to this day that his biological parents were praying for him. Needless to say, my mom and dad were unevenly yoked. The Bible warns of this and I think it was a huge reason for all we went through as a family. My mom wanted to raise us to love and serve the Lord, and my dad wasn't against it, he just didn't want to be bothered. And that caused spiritual warfare. My parents were divided and what my oldest sister was dabbling with and going through opened pandoras box.

My dad was easy-going, and my mother was more of a disciplinarian. Dad would discipline but he had a soft heart, so we could easily get him to lessen our punishment. I do have a few memories of running from the belt, which in my opinion was a good thing. My parents just weren't in agreement all the time and because of that, we knew how to break them down. This caused instability and that, combined with spiritual warfare, created chaos.

Let us journey on.

Chapter Two

Introduction to the Enemy

Our home life that was loving and content became an environment of complete chaos and turmoil. There was so much fighting and dysfunction. My father, mother, and my oldest sister, Shannon, would be up until the late hours of the night fighting and this was a regular occurrence. The death of our grandmother seemed to trigger Shannon's destructive behavior as they were extremely close. Shannon thought of her as a second mother; especially because she and our mother were not close at this time. There was an unexplained separation between them. Things went from bad to worse fast and there seemed to be no end in sight.

I can't tell you how many times my mom would tell me to lock my bedroom door at night because they didn't know what my sister Shannon was capable of. My parents thought she was possessed. She became involved with the wrong crowd and was already an alcoholic and into drugs. The late 70s and early 80s music of hard rock had a demonic push, many bands and songs were pushing 666, the number of the beast, and glorifying Satan. Shannon and a couple other girls in the neighborhood were also playing with a Ouija board. With everything else happening in our home, it was the perfect storm.

Shannon said that she hated God for taking her grandmother—and this is so hard to write—she invited Satan into her life.

Things got seriously out of control one night. I remember Shannon running up the stairs and shouting obscenities; she was angry and unrestrained. My father, mother, and my older brother, Jimmy, ran up the stairs after her. I remember being at the foot of the bed looking on as my mom and brother held Shannon down from the left side of the bed and my father held her down from the right side, as she was kicking and flailing and screaming. Then, all of a sudden, she stopped, turned her head toward my mom, and said, "I'm going to Hell and he especially wants you!".

My mother immediately said, "I rebuke you in the name of Jesus, and I am not going to Hell, nor is she!". While saying this, my mom made the Sign of the Cross with her hand. This is all I can remember from that night. I didn't know until a few years ago that my sister Jeanne, the middle sibling five years older than me, was standing to the left of me when this was happening, and my sister Laurel, who is two years older than me, was in the room at the end of the hall. As a six-year-old child, I was too young to understand what was happening, but I was skeptical about my sister being possessed. I thought it was probably just anger and alcohol speaking. I will soon share the experience that opened my eyes and made me no longer a skeptic.

When thinking of the movies *Poltergeist*, or *The Exorcist*, we think of possession, but possession comes in many forms. Remember, too, that Satan isn't dumb and knows if he shows that form of possession, all will believe he exists. He wants us to think he does not exist, that Hell does not exist, and everyone goes to Heaven.

Let's journey on.

Chapter Three

Life Can Be Overwhelming

After the "possession" experience with Shannon, I remember people from the church coming in and praying over every door and window in our house. It seemed like everything was falling apart. My dad lost his job with State Government and was working five jobs to make ends meet. I sensed even at a young age that my parents were struggling with their marriage also. I know my brother was giving them some issues that were normal for a teenager. When it rains, it pours.

I remember shopping at the Salvation Army and getting assistance for meals at school. I would go out with my dad on one of his jobs delivering papers in the early hours of the morning. I have so many memories of dogs chasing me at apartment complexes, and having to jump on a car to stop the dog from biting me. One day we pulled into a corner store and a sign on the window said, DONUT 25 CENTS. I said, "Dad, can I get a donut?" My dad gently grabbed my leg and said, "Son, we don't have money for that."

I learned so much in those years of struggling as a family. My dad taught me that a man does whatever he needs to support his family, even working five jobs. I also learned if you want something, you better work for it because it will not be handed to you. Those years shaped me for life. I will never forget where I came from, and I have compassion for those who struggle. I would not change what I learned going through that time; those lessons taught me how to handle life.

I feel I adjusted well with my chaotic childhood, but I also had some struggles. I struggled in school with reading and was held back in first grade. I now realize that I suffered with Attention Deficit Disorder (ADD). I hated school and couldn't wait till the day I was done with it. When I was reading, my mind was on the playground. I could read well, but had trouble comprehending what I was reading. I was excellent with math, but anything related to reading comprehension was hard because my mind was always racing.

Because we were financially struggling for a long period of time, I was encouraged to work. My parents did not have extra money to give us. So, at seven and eight years old I would go door-to-door looking for jobs. I remember shoveling my neighbor's large driveway for $2 during a big storm. For a little kid, that was pretty good to shovel a whole driveway without help. I was blessed by God with great work ethics, which my dad taught me by example. I pushed my mower down the street 3/4 of a mile to mow a lawn for $6, I mowed another lawn that was big but closer to my house for $8. This taught me that responsibility and hard work paid off. Years later I started a landscaping business and was very successful. I would not want to struggle through those issues again, but I know they helped mold me into the person I am today. As chaotic as our house was, my parents were loving and raised us right. Were they perfect? No, but who is? I thank God for my parents.

Before we get into how God dealt with my skepticism, I want to describe the day that crushed our family and negatively impacted me in many ways. I should have received counseling because I believe I've lived with Post-Traumatic Stress Disorder for most of my life, but God has shown me how to deal with it within the last ten years since I've drawn closer to Him.

Let's journey on.

Chapter Four

A Day of Huge Loss

I t was a beautiful fall day, September 25, 1985. I was twelve years old. I remember getting off the bus and walking to the house not knowing what I was about to be told. My parents met me at the door and by the look on their faces, I knew something wasn't right. In my mind I was thinking they were going to tell me something bad about my dad. I always had a fear of losing my dad, probably because he smoked and drank, plus, my parents were under a lot of stress because of all they went through with my sister, in addition to other life issues.

My parents sat me down and told me my brother Jimmy was killed tragically in an accident at the Heritage Ball Park that morning. He was working for a local contractor digging a ditch to install piping and the contractor didn't put wall braces up to protect the walls from caving in. One of my brother's friends, Timothy Anatriello, dug him out but it was too late. A metal slab from above fell and hit him in the chest and severed his aorta, the main valve to the heart. The coroner later told my mom he died instantly and didn't suffer, even though he had brain waves two hours later at the hospital.

When my parents told me the news, I was crushed and so overwhelmed. I did not know what to do with my feelings. The emotions were crippling. My big brother...I would never see him again! He was in a lot of ways my hero. I would never be able to hug him, love him, look to him for advice or protection. I loved my brother, I looked up to him; he was strong, loving, and enjoyable to be around. I remember crying till no tears came out anymore. It was so hard to comprehend that someone who had been there my entire life was gone, that I would never see him again on this earth. I was devastated!

There were over 500 people at my brother's wake and funeral. I will never forget the never-ending line of people. I remember being beside the casket touching his mustache. I think I was in shock trying to comprehend that my brother was gone. There was so much love and support during the wake and funeral, but after it was over it seemed everyone disappeared, and we were expected to "get back to life." I felt such pain from this massive loss, and I could not imagine going back to my normal life. I remember struggling with that and thinking, *I'm just supposed to go back to normal?* I felt like my life would never be normal again so please try to support those you love in the days after funeral services. The loss of a loved one is unimaginable, and the grief and loneliness can make them feel trapped. They need all of the continued support that they can get. Everyone grieves differently and we need to be sensitive to that. Don't worry about what to say because you don't need to say anything, just be there. Sometimes a gentle hug is all that's needed, or crying with them. Love conquers all. Jimmy passed away in Fall and I didn't notice until years later that every time I was around mums, which are fall flowers, it would bring me back to that terrible day. It's incredible how a smell can trigger a memory, but when I think of the flowers by his grave, it all comes together. As I write this, it stirs up such emotion even now, thirty-five years later.

People say that "time heals" and I believe that over time we learn to cope with loss, but not a day goes by that I don't think of my brother and long to one day see him again in Heaven. As I sit here, in front of me is something special that God used to comfort my heart—a picture of Jesus holding a young man who looks exactly like my brother. Every little detail in this picture resembles my brother. The picture is called, *Welcome Home*. Words cannot convey how much it means to me. I am so thankful to the Zuelsdorfs, close friends of our family, who listened to the promptings of God *prior* to my brother's death while they were on vacation. The Lord told them to purchase the picture, that they would need it in the future. This is how God uses people to fulfill His purpose. The Zuelsdorfs, such an amazing people and followers of God, were His hands and feet that day. Shortly after my brother passed away, they realized who the picture was for and presented it to us. Little did they know what that picture would do for me and my family. (Matthew 5:41): *"Blessed are those who mourn, for they will be comforted."*

I want to share something that God showed me about my brother. I was reading the Bible one day and came across 1 Corinthians 6:10: *"Nor thieves nor the greedy nor drunkards nor slanderers nor swindlers will inherit the Kingdom of Heaven."* As I read that, a panic came over me. Was my brother in Heaven? My brother was killed just two months before his twenty-first birthday, he was just a kid, and I know he really wasn't living a typical Christian life. As this panic was in my heart I prayed to God and asked, "Is my brother with you?" God answered me with this poignant memory of my brother when he got kicked out of the house because he was not obeying the rules. He came over on a Sunday night to have dinner with us and as he was leaving my mother grabbed him by his big puffy jacket (it was winter) and said, "Jimmy, if you were to die tonight, do you know where you would go?" He said, "Yes, Mom, I would go to Heaven." She grabbed his jacket tighter, pulled him in, and said, "Why?" Jimmy said, "Because I believe in Jesus Christ as my Lord and Savior."

God gave me that memory to show me my brother was with Him. In a later chapter I share how God affirmed this to me again one amazing day when He used me to be His hands and feet in a very special way. The Zuelsdorfs were prompted by God to purchase the picture for our family prior to my brother's death, and then my grandfather sent us a letter that Jimmy wrote to him and it said that he accepted Jesus Christ as his Lord and Savior—these were the ways God showed me that my brother was with Him. This is how amazing God is and how He comforts us in His own special way.

If there is someone reading this now who is struggling with grief over the loss of a loved one, I pray that God overwhelms you with His presence. James 4:2: *"You have not because you ask not."* Pour your heart out to God and ask him to give you clarity and comfort—He will! He is an amazing, loving, faithful God! If you don't know Him, my prayer is that you will by the end of this book.

Let's journey on.

Chapter Five

The End of Skepticism

It was an ordinary day that shaped my life and I never realized it till many years later. I was at the top of the stairs in the hallway when I looked down at my sister who was in the rocking chair in the family room at the bottom of the stairs. As I yelled down to ask her something, she turned around, looked up at me, and as our eyes met, her face disappeared and morphed into a demon. It could have been Satan himself looking at me with a smirk on his face and instantly in my head, I heard, *"I still have ahold of her."* At first, I was in shock and then the fear of what I was looking at set in and I jumped back behind the wall that led to the upstairs bedroom, frozen in fear. I was too afraid to move and wondered if what I just saw was still looking at me or drawing closer to me. Words can't express the pure evil I saw. As I was frozen in fear, I could hear my mom in her bedroom down the hall going through her drawers. I yelled in a stage whisper to my mom, not wanting the demon to hear or see me. My mom finally came out and I was still hiding behind the wall and told her what I saw. My mom yelled down to my sister telling her what I said, and she laughed it off. I don't believe my sister even realized what happened to her.

One thing I learned from that day that if is there is a Devil, there is a God!

I never really thought about what the Lord allowed me to see. Maybe I was exposed to so much that I became desensitized and didn't realize the significance of it at the time, or maybe God knew I wasn't ready for its purpose. Many, many years later, He would pull the veil from my eyes and give me understanding of what I witnessed that day. In the Book of Ephesians 6:12, the Apostle Paul says, *"For we wrestle not against flesh and blood, but against principalities, against powers, against the rulers of darkness of this world, against spiritual wickedness in high places."* God allowed me to see in a realm that is invisible to the eye. I have learned so much from that experience that it burdens my heart for the lost.

For one, so many people don't believe in Hell, and so many believe everyone goes to Heaven. This is exactly what Satan wants you to think. If you believe that, he's got you exactly where he wants you. They say people spend more time planning a vacation than planning where they will spend eternity. We are in a spiritual battle here on earth and if you are not fighting, you have already lost the war. There is a Devil with legions of demons who come to rob, torment, kill, and destroy. They want to destroy you and your family and do everything in their power to keep you from the One who sets you free—Jesus Christ.

One day my wife and I were watching *Unsolved Mysteries* and the episode was about a young couple who unknowingly rented a haunted house. Strange things started to happen and then got worse, with drawers flying across the room and pure evil running wild. The couple abandoned the house, left all their belongings, and never looked back. I remember my wife and I saying we would have been out of that house right away. But I also remember pondering why our house never got that chaotic, and I asked God why. I felt the Lord answer, *"Thus far, no further."* My mom represented Jesus so Satan was only allowed to go so far.

If you feel stressed or fearful right now, don't! (John 4:4): *"Ye are from God, little children, and have overcome them: because greater is He that is in you, than he that is in the world."* "He that is in you" is Jesus and "He that is in the world" is Satan. If you have never invited Jesus into your heart, take the time right now to do so. (2 Corinthians 6:2): *"Today is the day of salvation."* This is a prayer you can use:

> *Dear God, I know I am a sinner and confess my sins to you. Jesus, I believe you died for my sins and rose from the dead, I believe you are the Son of God. Please forgive me and I invite you, Jesus, into my heart to be Lord and Savior of my life. Please guide my life and help me walk in your ways.*

****

One thing I learned from that day with my sister is that Satan has the power to speak to us. They say there are three voices in your head: God's, yours, and Satan's. I have listened to shows and heard stories of people who have tried to commit suicide and failed, thankfully. Many have said the voices in their heads told them to do so. I remember hearing a documentary on the Son of Sam serial killer, David Berkowitz, who is now a born-again Christian. This man has been set free through Jesus is a genuine man of God now and you can watch his testimony on You Tube. He has said the voices in his head would tell him to kill people and the dark presence would overcome and take control of him. Our minds are the biggest battlefield we face on this journey called life.

Second, possession comes in many forms. Yes, it can be as serious as the movie, *The Exorcist,* but that is extremely rare. Satan knows if everyone sees this kind of possession like the movie, they will believe he exists. Most are snared. (2 Timothy 2:26): *"Then they will come to their senses and escape from the trap of the devil, who has taken them captive to do his will."*

There are many forms of possession, and it can manifest in different ways, such as rage, racism, division, brutality, rape, murder, etc. I don't have all the answers, but I have analyzed that roots of undealt bitterness and unforgiveness are what give Satan ground and can lead to possession. This over time can harden the heart so much it blocks the voice of God. Yes, some very hurtful circumstances take time to heal from and some are so deep and hurtful that you need God's help, but if you hold onto this and refuse to deal with it, you are giving Satan an open door to your life. Also, when we are bitter and hold onto unforgiveness, we hurt ourselves most of all. Not all who hold onto this will be possessed, but it's a very dangerous door to be left open. Obviously, playing with witchcraft and inviting Satan in is opening a door. There are many situations that can open this door, but these examples are what have stood out to me. Jesus did it all. (1 John 4:4): *"Greater is He that is in us than he that is in the world."*

With Jesus Lord of your life, you are protected from Satan, but you must invite Jesus in.

If you are skeptical, let's take a slight detour on the journey and see if you are ready to have the Lord open your eyes. This next chapter is for the skeptic.

Chapter Six

Open My Eyes, Lord

This chapter is dedicated to the skeptic. Before we move on, I want you to know I respect you. I am a skeptic. I do not believe everything that I hear or am told. I research until the person, situation, or circumstance earns my trust; I scrutinize every detail. I don't want anything but the absolute truth. I am going to discuss our basic eye-openers under examination. Before we start, I urge you to shut-off your cell phone and anything else that will distract you. Satan's number one tool is discouragement, but I would say his second powerful tool is distraction. Now let's begin.

All time is measured on Jesus Christ's existence—before His death (BC) and after His death (AD). Have you ever given any thought to this? This is how concrete Jesus' existence and crucifixion was and is. We know Jesus existed, it has been proven from history. The question for many of you is: Is he the Son of God? Well, let's start with the prophecies in the Old Testament about Jesus coming and being the Messiah (Savior) of the world:

(Isaiah 7:14): *"The Messiah would be born of a virgin."*

(Daniel 2:44): *"The Messiah throne will be anointed and eternal."*

(Isaiah 9:6): *"For unto us a child is born, to us a son is given; and the government shall be upon His shoulders, and His name shall be called Wonderful Counselor, Mighty God, Everlasting Father, Prince of Peace."*

(Isaiah 53:5): *"But He was wounded for our transgressions, He was bruised for our iniquities: the chastisement of our peace was upon Him, and by His stripes we are healed."*

There are roughly 414 passages from the Old Testament given and discussed in the light of fulfillment in Jesus, the Messiah (store.biblearchaeology.org). The probability of all these prophecies coming through one person is near impossible; in fact, you would have a better chance at winning the lotto. But how do we know these prophecies were not written *after* Jesus was born? In 1949, the discovery of The Dead Sea Scrolls in Qumran was significant in corroborating evidence of the Old Testament Scriptures. The ancient texts found hidden in pots in clifftop caves by a monastic religious community confirm the reliability of the Old Testament text. Archaeologists have proven that these manuscripts predate the birth of Jesus (*Scientific Facts in the Bible* by Ray Comfort). There are many prophecies in the Old and New Testaments. Look at Israel being scattered and then brought back as a nation 2,000 years later, as prophesied. Incredible!

The Shroud of Turin, also called Holy Shroud, is the linen believed to be the burial garment of Jesus Christ. It has been preserved since 1578 in the royal chapel of the Cathedral of San Giovanni Battista in Turin, Italy. Years ago, an episode of the *Oprah* show featured a little eight-year-old girl, Akiane Kramarik, who drew an amazing picture of Jesus called "Prince of Peace". She said that Jesus visited her in dreams when she was three or four years old and when she was eight, she drew the picture of Jesus. Yes, you read that right—

eight years old. The giftedness of this little girl is a miracle, but the picture of Jesus is absolutely amazing and when lined up against the Shroud of Turin is almost 100 percent identical. Read the book or watch the movie, *Heaven is For Real*, about a little four-year-old boy, Colton Burpo, who died and went to Heaven. For years his parents would show him pictures of Jesus and the little boy would say, "No, that's not what He looks like," until one day he saw Akiane Kramarik's painting of Jesus and said, "That's Him." I believe this is God's way of giving you little nuggets of something tangible to grasp, but remember, it's faith you need. Faith is what pleases God.

****

Let's move on to the miracle of the Bible and its existence (http://www.britannica.com; The editors of Encyclopedia Britannica).

The Holy Bible is an absolute miracle given to us by God. Some call it God's love letter to us, and I would agree. The Bible was written over 1,600 years, by more than forty different authors, many complete strangers to one another. Some were poor, some were rich. Some were businessmen, shepherds, fishermen, soldiers, physicians, preachers, and kings—people from all walks of life from three different continents in three different languages. This is a miracle, and it comes together in complete agreement and with complete harmony (*Scientific Facts of the Bible* by Ray Comfort). The Bible is 100 percent accurate, so accurate that some historians and archaeologists use the Bible to reference or confirm research. Never has the Bible been proven wrong. All the men of the Bible were moved by the Holy Spirit and penned what God placed on their hearts.

(2 Peter 1:20-21): *"Knowing this first, that no prophecy of Scripture is of any private interpretation, for prophecy never came by the will of man, but holy men of God spoke as they were moved by the Holy Spirit."*

(2 Timothy 3:16-17): *"All Scripture is given inspiration of God, and is profitable for doctrine, for reproof, for correction, for instruction in righteousness, that the man of God may be complete, thoroughly equipped for every good work."*

Many people in history have tried to remove the Bible from society and none have been successful. French philosopher Voltaire, born in Paris, France, was an influential, prolific writer who hated Christianity and did everything in his power to attack and eradicate the Bible. He predicted the Bible would not exist within 100 years. Before he died he said, "My one regret in dying is that I cannot aid you in this noble enterprise, the finest and most respectable which the human mind can point out, of extirpating the world of this." He was so toxic to the Bible. It is said that a priest tried to get him to ask forgiveness, turn from sin, and accept God's love, but he refused. God's love for us is relentless, He will pursue us to our last breath. Voltaire had one last chance and refused the love of God. In my opinion only our pride and stubbornness can stop the love of God. The Bible warns that we can shut out the voice of God so much that our hearts harden.

(Hebrews 3:15): *"Today if you will hear His voice, Do not harden your hearts as in the rebellion."*

I love the saying, "You have to step over Jesus to get to Hell." Anytime we talk about Hell it should always be done with compassion. Voltaire's story saddens me deeply. Hell is complete separation from God, and this is scary! But it is our choice. Within fifty years of Voltaire's death, the house where he wrote his thoughts against God was used to store Bibles and religious pamphlets, and the printing press in that house was then used to print Bibles. God is patient and has a sense of humor. God will not be mocked!

(Galatians 6:7): *"Do not be deceived, God is not mocked; for whatever a man sows, that he will also reap."*

There's a saying, "The wheels of justice grind slowly, but they grind." The Bible is the most widely sold book each year and is God's miracle love letter to you (crossexamined.org).Voltaire

Let's move on to God's twelve Apostles.

****

Ten of the twelve Apostles were martyred for their faith in Jesus and His resurrection. They would not deny that Jesus was the Son of God and that He rose from the grave. If they did not physically see this with their own eyes, they would have never sacrificed and died agonizing deaths for it. The only Apostle to not be martyred was the Apostle John, who was exiled to the Island of Patmos where he wrote the Book of Revelation inspired by the Holy Spirit. You can travel to Rome and visit the Mamertine Prison where it is said the Apostle Paul spent his last years before he was martyred for his faith and claims in Jesus. You can travel to Chennai, India, where a large part of this region pays patronage to Doubting Thomas. They called him Doubting Thomas because he said he did not believe that it was Jesus, resurrected, unless he put his fingers in Jesus' side. Jesus allowed Thomas to put his fingers into his side.

(John 20:29): *"Jesus said unto him, 'Thomas, because thou hast seen Me, thou hast believed. Blessed are they that have not seen and yet have believed."*

Doubting Thomas' tomb is believed to be built beneath Gothic-style Santhome Cathedral. Some of the many relics from Thomas remain in Chennai, India, but some are also in Italy at the Vatican. The Apostle Peter's tomb is beneath St. Peter's Basilica. It is believed that the Apostle Peter was crucified upside down because he didn't feel worthy to be crucified the same way Jesus was. You can research on your own about each of the Apostles who were martyred.

Now on to Creation.

****

Right now, we are spinning a thousand miles an hour on the earth's axis. Yes, a thousand miles an hour. The sun is about ninety-three million miles from earth; if we were a foot or more closer we would burn up and if we were a foot or more away we would freeze. Think about how perfectly God designed our solar system. We were taught in school that Christopher Columbus sailed the ocean blue and figured out the world was round in 1492 (*Scientific Facts of the Bible* by Ray Comfort). And if we go back a couple thousand years to the Book of Isaiah, God states the world is round.

(Isaiah 4:22): *"It is He who sits above the circle of the earth."*

(Job 26:7): *"He spreads out the northern skies over empty space; He suspends the earth over nothing."*

Scientists did not discover that the earth is not supported in space until sometime in the 1600s. They have yet to make a Hubble Space Telescope that reaches the end of the galaxies. If you have time I suggest watching *Indescribable* by Louie Giglio. He does an amazing job showing earth and our galaxies; he has such a passion for this that his heart reaches yours. When you see how small earth is compared to our galaxy, you realize how small *we* really are, but it makes you feel in awe of God, our Creator. I never had any interest in space until I watched

Indescribable. All my life I took things for granted, but as you draw closer to God you realize how amazing and creative He is.

The next time there is a full moon, take a minute to look up. You'll notice how perfectly round the moon is, just as the sun is perfectly round. Notice the beauty and power of the ocean as the waves crash on the beach; the glistening of the sun as it hits the water of the lake; the mountains and their shapes, color, and beauty. Look at the beauty of a single rose. Seriously think about it. The computer you use, the TV you watch didn't just appear, there was a designer. The earth in all its beauty has a designer and is the only planet with a unique solar system that can support life with perfect temperatures and ecosystem to sustain life. God is absolutely amazing!

****

Let us move on to the greatest miracle of all—the human body.

(Psalms 139:13-14): *"For You formed my inward parts; You covered me in my mother's womb. I will praise You, for I am fearfully and wonderfully made; marvelous are Your works, and that my soul knows very well."*

We are God's living, walking miracles. Not only did God make and knit us together in our mother's womb, but He knows every hair on our heads.

(Luke 12:7): *"And even the very hairs of your head are all numbered."*

God backs this up with DNA. If you were to take a drop of your blood and have it examined under a microscope, not one person in this entire world of seven billion people would have the same genetic code. You can determine that your parents and siblings are related, but everyone's DNA has a different code. Not one person in this world has your fingerprint, toe print, or tongue print. If there was no designer our blood would just be red, with no DNA. Seriously, think about that. Not only is God amazing, but He's a God of love.

(1 John 4:7): *"Whoever does not love does not know God, because God is love."*

Consider the miracle of your heart that beats over a hundred thousand times each day and pumps two thousand gallons of blood through your veins. Your body is made up of hundreds of muscles, hundreds of bones, miles of nerve fibers that are beautifully and wonderfully made by your Creator. That blood, which we take for granted, is a miracle liquid which carries food and oxygen to every part of your body. You have blood cells that kill germs and attack harmful substances. Your blood has cells that will clot to save you from losing too much of it. Your blood regulates your temperature and maintains body fluids. Every second, millions of blood cells die and millions are regenerated. Blood vessels in an adult will stretch over one hundred thousand miles long.

Open your lungs and take in that fresh oxygen. You breathe over fifty thousand times a day without thinking about it. Your lungs take in oxygen and you exhale carbon dioxide. Your lungs protect your heart and help cool your body down. Your brain is the biggest wonder of the body and creation. Your brain weighs roughly three pounds and contains more nerve cells than there are people on earth. Each nerve cell in your brain is connected to hundreds of offshoots that look like branches and the information that it gives out is more complex than the computer programs of a major city. Your brain can store and exchange more information than a computer. We take this for granted. We are walking miracles, designed in the image of God, and are wonderfully and beautifully made.

A few more things to ponder: we all know the story of God parting the Red Sea for Moses and the Israelites to protect them from Pharaoh and his armies and when the Egyptians tried to pass through, God brought back the water. This got Moses and his people to dry, safe ground and stopped Pharaoh and his army dead in their tracks. Many of Pharaoh's army, horses, and chariots were engulfed by the Red Sea. Scientists have found chariots at the bottom of the Red Sea, along with many artifacts of the Egyptian army. (http://www.discovery.global/chariot-discovered-in-red-sea). You can watch videos of the discovery by going to duckduckgo.com-Pharaoh's chariots discovered.

In (Joshua 10:12), God stopped day from moving to give Joshua and his armies victory over the Amorites. So that Joshua and his armies could continue fighting by daylight, God not only stopped night from coming but also called down a powerful storm to crush their enemies. Many scientists to this day believe there is a period of time missing. When they sent the computer measurements for time back and forth over the centuries, it came up with a day short in time measurements (http://www.snopes.comfact-check/the-lost-day/). Folks, God is showing you He is our Creator and His word is true and eternal.

As we close out this chapter, I urge you to think about your life. I think we move at such a fast pace with so many distractions and travel the road of life not giving enough thought to who we are. We take for granted the miracle of being, of living on Planet Earth in this amazing galaxy, the beauty of a rising sun, a sky full of stars, a field of beautiful flowers, and the nice breeze on a hot summer day. God created us to commune with each other, and commune with Him for His glory.

(Isaiah 43:7): *"Everyone who is called by My name, Whom I have created for my glory; I have formed him, yes, I have made him."*

It was Pascal who said, "There is a God-shaped vacuum in the heart of each man which cannot be satisfied by any created thing but only by God the Creator, made known through Jesus Christ."

I pray this chapter through God's presence has helped you realize there is a God who laid down His Son for you. God's love is perfect, and perfect love has no demands. It is up to you to invite Jesus into your heart and spend time getting to know your Creator. I promise you will be so glad you did. Always remember, God is love, and He loves you.

Back to the journey.

Chapter Seven

The Storm Continues

If having your oldest daughter possessed and in trouble and then tragically losing your oldest son wasn't enough, my sister Laurel, who is 2 years older than me, picked up the baton of dysfunction with one bad decision after the other and then the tragic loss of our brother sent her on a downward spiral.

Laurel and I were extremely close and inseparable when we were younger and have so many happy memories of Jimmy, especially the times when he wrestled with both of us. The last interaction I had with him was three days prior when he spent time with me showing me how to shuffle a deck of cards. Our schedules were different so on the day of his death, I was still sleeping when he was getting ready for work. My sister Laurel and my mom remember the house being a little chaotic that morning with everyone rushing to get ready for their daily activities. We had seven people living in a house with one small full bathroom so you can imagine the scene. None of us knew that would be the last time we would see Jimmy but if we did, I'm sure that morning would have played out much differently. We had a lot of issues as a family, but we all loved each other and were close.

Always treat each moment as if it were your last. You never know when your last interaction will be with those you love. Resolve your conflicts because life is short and fragile. Part of love is forgiveness.

The Bible says our lives are like a breath, a mist, a vapor, and then we are gone.

Jimmy would often tell our mom that he was concerned that Laurel was heading in the wrong direction and possibly going down a road that could be more troubling than Shannon's. He was right, as hard as that was to comprehend. To this day, thirty-six years later, her life is in constant turmoil, dysfunction and heartbreak. We feel as a family that at any moment we could get a call informing us that she is gone. Obviously, we pray against it, but my most fervent prayer is that she gets her heart right with God before she passes. During Jimmy's funeral, she acted so peculiar, hanging out with her friends like nothing ever happened. I share that because it stood out to me, and I now understand that it was her way of dealing with the loss. She was in shock and everyone grieves differently. I have learned to be sensitive to that.

After the funeral she began skipping school and getting into trouble. She would soon run away, and we didn't know where she was for half a year or more. She ended up with Shannon and her friends. Shannon was living in a very bad section of Schenectady, about fifteen minutes away from our house. During that time, Laurel got hooked on crack-cocaine and would do anything for her next high which landed her in and out of jail. Crack-cocaine has a three percent cure rate. What does that mean? Only three out of every hundred people can recover from the disease, that's how addictive it is. Hate the disease, love the person!

Laurel now has three grown children but because of the severity of her addiction, she wasn't able to care for them when they were growing up so close friends and family stepped in to raise them. Laurel is such a beautiful person inside and out but unfortunately got caught up in something that took control over her life and she was powerless to stop it. I can't even count how many rehabs she went through, many she didn't finish, and the constant heartache this disease has put our family through. My heart breaks for Laurel as I know she has incredible pain and regret from her past. I truly believe every time she gets clean her past haunts her to the point that makes her run back to the drugs to numb for the pain; which in turn causes *more* pain. I love what the Apostle Paul says in (Philippians 3:13): *"No, dear brothers and sisters, I have not achieved it, but I focus on this one thing: forgetting the past and looking forward to what lies ahead."*

The Apostle Paul was, some say, the greatest Apostle, but in his earlier years he was also responsible for so many awful things done to the first Christians, even taking part in murdering them. Think about it—if he let his past ruin him like so many people do, he never would have become the greatest Apostle and achieved so much for Christ and been used so powerfully. You have to accept Christ's forgiveness and put the past behind you. If God forgives you, you must forgive yourself. There is nothing you have done that God won't forgive. That's the beauty of God—not only does He love us but He forgives us and no longer remembers our sins. One day when we stand before God we can only say one thing: "I trust in Jesus." Because of Jesus there is no condemnation, no judgment.

Jesus took our sins on the Cross. We cannot earn salvation; it is a gift so no one can boast (Ephesians 2:9). If we could earn salvation and buy our way into Heaven, then the agonizing death Jesus suffered on the Cross was for nothing. If that is you, if you have asked God for forgiveness, you need to accept His forgiveness. It is not God reminding you but Satan tormenting you. Satan wants you to hold onto your past! Let your past go and accept God's forgiveness. He has amazing plans for you! Put the past behind, put your hand in His, and strive for the goal! Always remember, God uses blemished, unqualified people to fulfill His purpose (look who's writing this book). There is hope for everyone.

I remember when we were at church one day and she asked me to pray for her. She started to cry as I talked to her. She said, "You don't know the things I have done." I know she has many regrets, so much remorse. The drugs and addiction have ruined and wasted so much of her life. But there is still hope for her. I shared with her that no matter what she has done, if she brings it before God and repents, she will be forgiven.

(1 John 1:9): *"If we confess our sins, He is faithful and just and will forgive our sins and purify us from all unrighteousness."*

(Psalm 103:12): *"As far as the East is from the West, so far has He removed our transgressions from us."*

We all have tremendous regret and remorse about things in our lives. I know I do—so many things I wish I could go back and undo or change. *God knows this.*

Let's move on to myself picking up the baton of dysfunction. I have to share everything so you can learn from my mistakes and all God has taught me. Are you ready? Let's go!

Chapter Eight

My Baton of Dysfunction

I think every child wants to fit in and be accepted. We want to be cool and we want everyone to like us. It's human nature. I've had many childhood friends from all spectrums of life, but I gravitated to those doing the same things I watched my brother and sisters doing. When I was twelve I got involved with a group of kids and we all became close friends, like brothers. We used to call ourselves The Warriors. We got that from the movie, *The Warriors*. It was about street gangs fighting other gangs in New York City. Unfortunately, we started doing things we shouldn't be doing—drinking, smoking cigarettes, and smoking pot. We were some serious little rascals, but these guys became like family. I loved them like brothers, and I still do, even though we separated for a while. One member of our gang died a year or so ago from cancer, but everyone else is carrying on with life.

One night transformed my life. I was fourteen. I was sick with bronchitis and I was smoking so many cigarettes and so much pot that I couldn't breathe. I don't want to be too graphic but I remember hanging over the sink hacking and the stuff I was spitting out was pure black. I knew if I asked my mom to bring me to the doctor, the doctor would tell her I was smoking. So, not being able to breathe, I propped five pillows under me and I remember saying a prayer to God, "If you let me live through the night, I will change my life for you tomorrow." All that dragging me to church and Sunday school sunk in. That's one of the reasons I am thankful my mom never stopped bringing us to church even though we fought with her and gave her so much trouble. Well, the next morning I woke up and followed through on what I told the Lord. I quit my bad habits and Jesus started to transform my life. When you invite Jesus in, He changes you from the inside out.

It is amazing what God can do. The hardest of criminals, even murderers, can be transformed. I love the story of serial killer Stephen Morin and Margy Palm, which is a great example of this. You can find the story on YouTube—listen to Margy Mayfield Abduction Testimony—it's 38 minutes and 20 seconds long. Be sure you listen to the very end, the story will move you. It is a testimony of God's incredible love for all.

****

One day, while hanging out with my friends at the market, I took candy from the store and was outside just about to start eating it, when the Holy Spirit convicted me. It was like Jesus was saying, *"I live here now and you're not eating candy you didn't pay for with Me here."* I didn't open it and I went into the store and put it back, stressing out that I might get caught returning it. It was so hard to pull away from my friends who were like brothers, but after that I became involved in church and we grew distant. I joined the church youth group and started to make new friends. I was on fire for God! I look back at this time and can see God's hands of protection on my life.

I was at a party and my sister Laurel stopped over. I can remember sniffing two lines of cocaine which she exposed to me. I thank God to this day it didn't kill me and believe if I had become addicted, my life would have been ruined. A few years later a couple of the kids we hung out with got caught doing more serious things. I remember this guest speaker, 24 years old, just out of prison, came and spoke to our congregation. He said, "You are one decision away from ruining your life." Think about that? One decision can ruin your life. Very true statement, but even scarier thought. They say sin will take you further than you want to go, keep you longer than you want to stay, and cost you more than you can pay. Well, I dropped the baton of dysfunction and decided to walk with God.

Let's travel down the road of God's amazing grace and forgiveness.

Chapter Nine

God's Beginning Path

I was on fire for God. I got very involved in church and one of the kids I met in the youth group, Eric, quickly became a close friend. His family would become close friends with my family and eventually would adopt my one niece, my sister Laurel's middle daughter. Laurel at this time was fully under the control of her addiction. As many have seen, the ramifications of addiction make it hard enough to take care of yourself let alone a child. She couldn't ask for a better family to adopt her daughter. They all care for each other and get along well, which is very rare to see these days.

Our youth group had a lot of fun and we were all growing in the Lord. Some were there because they had to be, but most were trying to be closer to God. God was moving in my life and I was getting to know the Lord but because I was a new Christian and so young, I was still being pulled back by what I thought I was missing. I was working a lot once I turned sixteen to pay for my car. I think I struggled with the Christian walk, which can be hard at times when you feel like you are under constant attack. If there's anything I do for new Christians, it's to prepare them for the battle they are in for. So many Christians live a defeated life because we don't practice what we preach.

(1 John 4:4): *"Greater is He that is in me than he that is in the world."*

(Romans 8:37): *"No, in all these things we are more than conquerors through Him who loved us."*

(Jeremiah 29:11): *"I know the plans I have for you, plans to prosper you and not to harm you, plans to give you hope and a future."*

We as Christians need to practice spiritual disciplines regularly to be successful in walking with God. Reading and studying His word daily, worship and praise, joining small groups, attending church, and our devotional time alone with God, are all wonderful practices.

Two to three years after giving my life to the Lord, I slid back into a life not pleasing to God. Feeling like things were always going wrong, combined with the thought that I would never find a girlfriend, made me impatient, and I took my life back into my hands. But God has a perfect will for our lives if we give Him the wheel and abide and trust in Him. God is always faithful, even when we are not. I will share what God has taught me about how the way we think causes much of our own demise. We need to correct our destructive thinking patterns.

For years my walk would be up and down like a roller coaster, and I would feel the demonic attacks. I think I always struggled with slight depression, not that people would notice. I love interaction with people most of the time, but I also love solitude. Sometimes you cannot see a person's inner struggles. I carried so much baggage from my childhood, as we all do. My childhood wasn't bad but the things we went through as a family created issues.

They say a child is shaped for life between the ages of three and nine years old. During those years we were dealing with my oldest sister being possessed and constant chaos in the house. My parents almost lost the house due to my dad losing his job, and because of that my parents would constantly be arguing about money in front of us. A few years later, the tragic loss of my brother and six months prior to that the loss of our childhood dog, and issues with my sister Laurel, added to the chaos. My dad's health was always a concern too.

Some baggage helps you navigate life, but some weighs you down. Part of the experience helped me because I became responsible with money, but I think it turned me into a workaholic because of the fear of not having enough or being able to provide for my family. Money was always a stress to me and I never wanted to experience financial strain again.

The tragic loss of my brother caused me to look at life differently. You live in fear of going through that pain again and would do anything possible to avoid another tragedy, especially to someone you love. I know I had Post-Traumatic Stress Disorder. I would be in a room full of people and rather than enjoy the moment I would think, *Who's next to die?* Going through that pain of losing someone you love shows you how fragile life is. Everything I went through with my sister—the constant turmoil in the house, worrying about my dad having a heart attack from his smoking, drinking, the stress of losing our house, financial troubles, and the tragic loss of my brother—created a negative thought pattern.

At this time, I started reading and it consumed me. The job I had allowed me the opportunity to read during down time, and when we would go on vacation I would read constantly. God was bringing books into my life that would change my destructive way of thinking. He was getting all the garbage out of my head. Think of your mind as a garden. If you plant tomatoes, you will grow tomatoes. If you plant cucumbers, you will grow cucumbers. You plant poison ivy, you will grow poison ivy. Why would you plant poison ivy? Why would you plant negative thoughts? The Bible says, (Proverbs 23:7): *"As a man thinks, so he is."* God was showing me through reading and sermons that if you plant negative thoughts, you will create negative emotions, and negative emotions lead to depression. You must create or plant positive thoughts and those positive thoughts will lead to positive emotions. Positive emotions lead to happiness.

Happiness is a choice. I had to stop living in the past and like the Apostle Paul said, put the past behind you and strive for the goal. When those negative thoughts come to you, immediately replace them with a positive thought.I heard John Maxwell quote this in a sermon." Don't resist, replace! What you resist comes at you stronger, so *replace*." This takes time because you are shaking a bad habit, getting rid of the "junk" that's been in your mind for years. Think of it as rebooting a computer, which is your mind and your thoughts. This helped me with the depression, but I now needed victory with the spiritual part. One of the things you will learn if you walk with God is that spiritual warfare is real.

Once you are a child of God, you are always His.

On to the backsliding. Let's journey on.

Chapter Ten

My Backslidden Journey

I quickly went back to hanging out with my old friends. I also had another group of friends and my childhood close friend, Sean. I introduced them all to each other. Our group was growing. I made a promise to God that I wouldn't smoke cigarettes or pot and I have kept that promise. I have literally woken up in a sweat with nightmares of breaking that promise. Dreams can be so real and sometimes when you wake up you're so thankful it was just a dream. I do believe God uses dreams to guide us...or warn us. I don't believe *every* dream has meaning. But God uses dreams in many people of the Bible: Joseph, Pharaoh, Nebuchadnezzar, and others.

Speaking of dreams, I have occasional nightmares that I am back in school. It's funny how we change. I hated school and as I mentioned earlier, I did not read any books until I was in my late thirties. I found a way of getting through every book report without reading the book. I remember renting the movie, *To Kill a Mockingbird,* to get that book report done. Nothing I'm proud of, I just had zero interest in school and reading. Now I love to read. That's why I said God really does have a sense of humor, guiding me to be an author!

I gave up pot and cigarettes but I started drinking. Most of my backsliding was running from God. I no longer was involved in church activity or spending time with God. I would go to church periodically but not consistently. I wanted my will over His. In eleventh grade I started dating Kim. We were very serious and were voted Homecoming King and Queen. In twelfth grade she became pregnant. We were just kids. I graduated in January of my senior year. I wanted to get out of school as soon as possible.

Kim and I got married the day after graduation from high school and we went on a cruise to Bermuda for our honeymoon. Kim was six and a half months pregnant at the time. When we returned, she became very sick with a temperature of 105.8 and she was hospitalized. While in the hospital, she started having trouble breathing and her blood oxygen level went to 30 percent. She was going septic and her lungs were filling with fluid. I remember the doctors piercing her lungs and draining the fluid from them but as fast as the fluid was draining, it was filling up again. No matter what the doctors tried, nothing was working, and Kim was dying. I remember the doctor saying to Kim, "If it comes down to you or the baby tonight, who do you want us to try to save?" She didn't even give it a thought, she said, "Save my baby." I was floored! She was only eighteen, still just a child herself—so brave but without even seeing that baby was willing to lay down her life for her. If there is any kind of human love that compares to God's love, it's a mother's love for her child. There is something about a mother's love, and that bond. I've often told those expecting their first child, "When you have a child you realize what love truly means, you realize how much you can love something, no greater love a human can have." I had an employee of mine come back to work after his child was born and tell me he now understands how true that statement is. With lots of prayer, and the grace of God, my wife and our oldest daughter made it through the crisis.

Because we were so young, our marriage was a constant struggle. I remember trying to find my way in life. I was working jobs for health benefits. I remember working for a local company and they wanted to promote me to a store in a bad section of Albany—a worker at that store was killed years prior in a robbery. I met the district manager at that store along with a few other men in management. I declined the promotion primarily because it was so far to travel. The district manager made me feel worthless; he belittled me in front of the other two managers and said, "Who are you to decline this promotion?" I was shocked because I thought he would be encouraging. I didn't say anything because my parents raised me to respect authority. I think that's why I didn't speak up, plus I was only nineteen at the time, and I was caught off guard. I drove home from there overwhelmed and feeling like a failure.

I needed to provide for my family and it was such an uphill battle. Then the anger set in. My dad always used to say, "Put manners on people," meaning, speak up and put people in their place if they are out of line. I ended up writing a letter to the corporation, we had a meeting with the district manager, and he apologized for his actions. I share that because I know how it is to feel like a failure, and I learned so much from that day. I think that's why I always try to encourage people in jobs you know aren't very rewarding, or if they seem to be at a crossroad in their lives.

People do not realize what a little encouragement or an act of kindness can do for someone. It moves mountains. I always remember all of the times that I've struggled, so I have compassion for those who are there. Life's trials are a learning experience and we must learn from them. Of course, it's always better to learn from someone else's mistakes if possible.

Shortly after that experience, I was able to get a job with a great company part-time with full benefits, and I decided to build up my lawn business. I was working from 6:30 a.m. to 10:30 p.m. every day doing hard physical labor. I would be so exhausted when I got home I would practically pass out. Because of the long hours, being so young and raising an infant, Kim and I grew apart. I can remember one night coming home and she said, "You don't love me anymore." I remember being so exhausted I didn't even know how to respond or have the energy to respond. The way we were living I could understand her feeling that way. We were just kids thrown into stresses and life issues beyond our years, not knowing how to balance it out. I had to pay for an apartment, vehicles, health insurance, groceries, and many other expenses—all at nineteen years old. Needless to say, the marriage ended in divorce.

Let's journey on.

Chapter Eleven

The Divorce

I remember my friend being in my truck and for some reason I had to drop Kim, my soon-to-be ex-wife off somewhere. After she got out of the truck and walked away, I told my friend, "I hate her." That's how much hurt and anger I was feeling at the time. I'm sure she felt the same way. How did we get there?

It was such a painful time in my life. I remember losing ten pounds and going out to bars every night of the week just trying to numb the pain and thinking another girl would be the cure. I remember one early morning driving to work at 3:30 a.m. for the preload shift raising my hand to God, tears streaming down my face, and saying, "How could You let this happen?" As if it was God's fault. Actually, if I were going to church and spending time with God at that time, I bet there's a good chance we would never have gotten divorced. Listen to (Proverbs 19:3) People's own foolishness ruins their lives, but in their minds they blame God.

One day after work, I stopped at my dad's house. I just needed someone to talk to. My dad greeted me at the door, wrapped his arms around me, and just cried with me for a good five minutes. At that point in life, words would not have helped. It was the most meaningful moment with my dad and meant so much—him holding me and crying with me. My dad's overwhelming love for me dulled the pain I was going through. If God gave me just that one moment with my dad, it would have been enough. Love conquers all! Just thinking back to that day makes me well up with emotion.

I remember still including Kim in my prayers and decided I was not going to pray for her anymore. Shortly after that, I dreamed that she died and I woke up crying and felt the Lord say to me, *"That's why you still pray for her."* God was telling me I still loved her. I believe in most divorces that the two people love each other but let walls of hurt, bitterness, and unforgiveness get in the way. You can be angry or hurt by someone but that doesn't stop your love for that person. I wouldn't wish divorce on my worst enemy, it's an awful thing to go through. I remember going to a psychologist who was a customer of mine and all he could say was, "The marriage never should have happened because you were so young." That was terrible counseling, and I had to pay for it. Needless to say, one visit was enough. I struggled with not being able to move on. I understand now, but then I couldn't see what was in the future, what God's plan was.

This whole experience, though, has created compassion in me—my heart breaks for anyone going through such a painful time. I love helping people who are struggling in marriage by guiding them to resources that helped me. If God could heal our marriage, he could heal any marriage. Kim and I were divorced for roughly four years. The first three years I went to bars all the time trying to drown the pain. I dated numerous girls. If there is one regret during that time, it was how I unknowingly misled so many girls, wasting their time making them think I was ready for a relationship. Not that they lost sleep over it. It had nothing to do with them, my heart belonged to someone else and I didn't even realize it. I was just too prideful to admit it, and the bad feelings were choking out the good. I wasn't yet healed and I believe God wouldn't let me move on because he knew the future. Little did we know my mom and Kim's mom were praying for us. After a few years of bars and girls, I finally got burned out and learned to stay home and do more constructive things with my time. I worked on more quality time with our daughter.

Roughly four years after we divorced, my close friends Ronnie and Tommy lost their father tragically from a heart attack. It was such a huge loss for their family. He was an excellent father and kept order in his house. I admired this man, and love their family. Kim and I went to the services together and ended up staying together. Seven months later we remarried. Our mothers were elated! God had answered their prayers. In October of 2024, we will be celebrating our 25th wedding anniversary!

There is power in prayer. When you don't see or think God is working, He is. Remember, God is faithful even when we are not.

I want to take another detour into the future and share all that God has taught me about marriage. No, I don't know it all, no, my marriage isn't perfect, but Kim and I love each other and we enjoy each other's company. I look forward to spending time with her whether going out to dinner, watching a movie, or going away for a weekend. We rarely argue and I think the longer you are with someone the more you adapt, but I also believe when you spend time with God and ask— (James 4:2): *"You have not because you ask not."*—God steps in and shows you how to be the husband or wife He called you to be, what your husband or wife needs you to be, and you desire to be. God is amazing!

Let's take that detour.

****

Ninety-nine percent of us read this Bible verse at our weddings:

(1 Corinthians 13:4-8): *"Love suffers long and is kind; love does not envy; love does not parade itself, it's not puffed up; does not behave rudely, does not seek its own, is not provoked, thinks not evil; does not rejoice in iniquity, but rejoices in truth; bears all things, believes all things, hopes all things, endures all things. Love never fails."*

Read that three times throughout the day and do everything in your power with the help of God to make this a part of your marriage. If every person in the world followed this, that would be a touch of Heaven! Love conquerors all!

On this journey God brought the book, *The Five Love Languages*, by Dr. Gary Chapman, into my life. This author is a gift from God—let me reiterate that—an absolute gift from God. I have given thirty to fifty of these books as gifts. God has healed a deep hurt in my life and has made it a burden for me to help others, and I believe Chapman's book is one of God's tremendous tools. This book is constantly on the bestseller list and I believe sells more each year than the previous year. This book also helps with your children's love language, which helped me with my son. Dr. Chapman has written several books dealing with relationships. I would like to share some things his book has taught me.

Many of my friends and family know I have struggled with "workaholism." My good friend Adam from childhood calls me the hardest-working guy in Colonie, the town we live in. I'm known for my work ethic; my dad was also a workaholic and I inherited that from him. I still work hard but I believe God has helped me learn to balance. Through drawing close to God, I feel the shackles of workaholism have been broken. I no longer feel guilty when I am not working. Work does not consume me anymore. I work hard but I take care of myself with rest and boundaries. Workaholism is admired but can be just as destructive as any other addiction. Addiction runs in our family and my sister who suffered from alcoholism would always say to me, "You got the good addiction." But my addiction has cost my family in many ways and has caused me regret in the loss of many special moments, because work took precedence over time I could have spent with them.

One day, during the second time around we were struggling in our marriage, I decided to send Kim flowers to the house. When I got home she just looked at me and said, "You don't get it." I was furious! I said, "I work so hard for you and this family, send you flowers, and I don't get it?" Dr. Chapman's book taught me that one of Kim's love languages, her dominant one, was *Quality Time*. Kim wanted me to spend quality time with her, because when I spend quality time with her, her "love tank" fills up and she feels loved. This is her primary way of receiving love and giving love. Sure, she likes flowers, but what she wants most is to spend time with me. My two love languages are *Affirmation* and *Physical Touch*. One day during the winter, this same period of time, I woke up in the morning suffering from a nasty cold and I was hacking over the sink. Kim came up behind me, rubbed my back, and asked if I was okay. It was like a lightbulb going on and I thought, *she does love me*! I receive love and give love by physical touch. When Kim is not getting the quality time she needs, she gets upset with whatever she feels is taking that quality time from her, which adds to the mess, because my love language (*Affirmation*) is not being filled and my love tank is being drained because we are not connecting.

This book helped me solve a huge piece of the puzzle, by encouraging me to identify mine and my spouse's love languages and how to meet them. I highly recommend Dr. Chapman's book, and I also suggest you listen to Jimmy Evans and his wife on marriage counseling. You can research them on YouTube. There are many good books and resources to help, and when you invite God in, He will guide you.

You should concentrate on your spouse's good points, not their shortcomings. No one is perfect. Any bad memories or thoughts come from the enemy. Remember, Satan is a tormentor and wants to ruin your marriage. Quickly replace negative thoughts with a good memory. I heard John Maxwell in a sermon share this. Whatever we resist comes at us stronger, so don't resist, *replace*. Focus on the good and block the bad.

Finally, focus on your marriage. If your marriage isn't happy, it affects everything. Your job will be harder, your relationships with your kids can be hindered, it affects everything. It's like a pyramid with your marriage being at the top. If the marriage is good, the benefits flow to all areas of your life. Picture a pyramid with God at the top and you and your spouse at the bottom. As you draw closer to God, you draw closer to each other. There have been many times Kim and I have argued and after going to prayer the Lord would say, *"You owe her an apology."*

When we spend time with God, He speaks to us, He guides us. We receive the fruits of the spirit—love, joy, peace, patience, kindness, generosity, faithfulness, gentleness, and self-control. Tell me that won't make your marriage better. If you put God first in your life by honoring Him, the blessings flow to your marriage, your family, your job, and your life. Ruth Bell Graham has said, "A happy marriage is the union of two good forgivers."

Make sure you and your spouse are spending quality time together, communicating and loving each other. Plan a date night, plan a weekend together, and I believe some time away can rekindle what was at the altar when you first said, "I do." We must treasure and have high regard for our marriage, our covenant before God. Marriage is sacred to God. God, the designer of marriage, holds it so precious that He uses this institution as a picture of His relationship with His Church. I need to cherish what I love. What God did for our marriage He can do for your marriage, and even if your marriage is good, protect it. Statistically, only one out of one-thousand marriages end in divorce if the spouses love and honor God and pray together daily.

As I close out this chapter, I pray that you invite Jesus into your life and ask Him to make your marriage what He the designer wanted it to be—a perfect union between a husband and wife filled with love, kindness, and compassion for one another. God is a miracle-working God and if He can heal our marriage, He can heal yours.

Let's journey on.

Chapter Twelve

We're a Family Again

K im and I remarried in 1999. In January of 2001, we had our son JonMichael. In May of 2004, we had our daughter Jillian. With our oldest daughter Devyn, we now had three children. Kim's pregnancy with Jillian at the end became life-threatening as well, and she became extremely sick again. Things got so stressful one night, and Kim's blood pressure dropped to 46/23; her health was in a critical state. I remember going into the bathroom and getting sick. That's how intense it was. Our whole family was at the hospital at 3:30 in the morning and John Wilson from our church, a beautiful man of God, showed up unexpectedly. We all gathered in prayer and poured our hearts out to God, and things took a dramatic turn for the better. The rest of the pregnancy went well. John Wilson represented Jesus, His hands and feet, that night; he was God's angel sent to us. We decided three kids would be enough after having two life-threatening pregnancies. I didn't want to lose my wife and raise children on my own.

We were living life and doing well. We had the normal struggles, but life was good. Around 2009, Kim and I felt a pull to go to another church. We decided to try a church in town, Grace Fellowship, which we heard many nice things about. It was such a difficult decision, we actually grieved leaving Our Savior's Lutheran Church. There were so many beautiful strong Christians there, and it was my childhood church and I had many memories growing up there. Our Savior's was where I came to really know God through the youth group and attending through adulthood. But we felt we needed something more at this season of our lives. It was like an inner eternal pull.

Grace Fellowship had more elaborate child care and many more resources available. Our children really fought us and didn't want to leave OSL. Sometimes Kim and I struggled wondering if we made the right decision. Our two youngest kids never got a chance to make their First Communion and Confirmation, but I do think it was God calling us to Grace Fellowship for a reason. Pastor Rex's preaching was so inspiring that it really made you want to pick up your cross and follow Jesus. Plus, he was so well-rounded, teaching how to live life in all aspects—marriage, parenting, relationships, discipleship, handling money, etc. God was really starting to move in my life.

I longed to get back to God the way I gave my life to him that scary night as a teenager. I would come out of Grace Fellowship Church after Pastor Rex preached, ready to take on the world for Jesus. Sometimes that hunger would end on the car ride home with an argument, sometimes it would last a day or two. I started to analyze how I could keep this hunger for God more consistent so it wouldn't die out. What was I doing wrong? I reached out and asked to meet with someone at the church to share my burden and discuss how I could fix my problem. I met with Warren DeLollo, a pastor in Missions. I told Warren my problem and I chuckle every time I think back to the conversation. Warren laughed in a friendly way and said, "Oh, this is easy. You just need to practice your spiritual disciplines," meaning, reading and studying the Bible daily, worship, prayer, joining small groups, etc. So, I worked on that, but with my demanding work schedule and raising a family I still struggled with consistency. I did well for a while but the pulls and demands of life made it a battle—a battle that would lead me to a pivotal part of my life—depression.

Let's journey on.

Chapter Thirteen

An Answer for My Depression

Why would I say that depression was a pivotal part of my life? I say that because it drove me to get answers, answers God would provide in such an intimate way.

I never really thought I struggled with depression. I think everyone can have circumstantial depression, but there really wasn't a cause for why I was feeling depressed, at least I couldn't think of any. My childhood wasn't normal in a traditional sense and it didn't seem to affect me emotionally, but as I look back I realize it did. I tend to analyze things to figure out why I feel the way I do or what was meant by an action or comment. Why was I feeling depressed? I had a beautiful wife, three beautiful kids, a nice house, a successful career with a good company, and a successful side business. What was the problem? This made no sense, and I'd never felt that way before. So, I reached out again to Warren DeLollo. If he weren't so gracious and kind the first time I met him, it could have stopped the way God was moving in my life. I hate inconveniencing anyone, I know the value of time, so if he wasn't so receptive to me, I never would have reached out to him again.

When I called Warren I shared what was going on and asked if he knew any good Christian counselors. I prefer a Christian certified counselor. They are certified like every other psychologist but their faith and relationship with God will also give them wisdom from above. Warren gave me three counselors' names and I remember asking, "Warren, out of these three, who do you suggest for me?" He gave it a quick thought and suggested this specific psychologist, and I quickly set up an appointment with the doctor.

I met Dr. B and after four visits she let me know that medications were an option in the process. I'm not against medication for other people, but I just knew it wasn't the answer for me. She asked if my wife would come in so it might help her better understand me. I told her Kim has always been against it because she'd seen so many people go through counseling and felt it never helped them, but I thought she would come in for me. I understand Kim's thoughts on this because she is looking at past performance of those she knew were counseled. I disagree with this viewpoint because it's what we choose to do with the counsel we receive, we have our responsibility to follow through. I think at some point in everyone's life it's wise to seek good counsel, and I mean *everyone*. Sometimes we just need someone to listen. I also believe people give up too soon before they experience a breakthrough.

Kim came in with me to the next visit but I felt like a punching bag during the entire session. I agreed with Kim on a lot of things she was saying. I'm a freak with my finances. Remember, my father lost his job when we were little, and I remember many arguments about money and losing the house. Those fears were ingrained in me from six to nine years old. I was so neurotic about money and finances that I never wanted to go back to financial periods of fear. I would do all I could to prevent that from happening.

I also carried the trauma of losing my brother tragically at twelve years old and that gut-wrenching pain. Six months before my brother died, I watched my childhood dog Muffin get hit by a truck—the guy in the truck actually sped up to hit her. To some that might not seem like much, but for those who have animals you realize you love them just like family members. Beginning when I was five years old, Muffin slept in my bed and everywhere I went she was right by my side. I can remember the fear on her face as she knew she couldn't get out of the way of that truck. After she got hit she lay lifeless on the edge of the road. I ran screaming, "*Muffin, Muffin!*" She tried to get up when she heard my voice but couldn't. We had to put her to sleep the next day. Thirty-five years later and I still remember the drive home crying uncontrollably after saying goodbye to our childhood dog, my best friend.

So, in 1985, the tragic loss of my brother and dog caused me to fear ever going through the loss of a loved one again. I would worry constantly, I would sit in a room and wonder who was next to die. I carried that fear over worrying about my kids. They had bronchitis and I worried it would kill them. A healthy tree branch was hanging over the swing set, I would cut it down to protect it from hurting them. My kids are sleeping at your house and if you didn't have smoke detectors I would install a few. And yes, I did install some at a friend's house so they could stay over. So, I understood Kim's gripes with me.

The night before the next visit that Kim came with me, I prayed to God. I prayed, "Lord, I signed up for this counseling but if tomorrow's visit goes anything like last week's visit, I'm done with this." The next visit was about thirty-five minutes in and I told Dr. B that I accepted a job that would enable me to work on my landscaping business more. I didn't like the job but I could spend more time reading. She said, "Jon, you are masking something." I said, "What do you mean by 'I am masking something'?" She said, "You are covering something up that's underneath." I was so overwhelmed with emotion I couldn't speak for a few minutes. It was like God came in the room and showed me that I was masking something I didn't even know was there. After I got myself together and could get the words out I said, "I feel God has a call on my life for which I am not fulfilling." It was like God gave me the words. Dr. B was moved and said, "I just witnessed a spiritual miracle." Dr. B now understood what my problem was, and so did I. It really was a miracle moment—a breakthrough. The way God works is amazing. Sometimes we want God to give us simple, instant answers, but the way He answers you, shows you how intimately He knows us. God used the doctor's gift for a miracle breakthrough moment.

Dr. B counseled me for two years as I drew closer to God. She was such an important part of the journey for which I am so grateful. I will always have respect and gratitude for how she helped me. I refer many people to Dr. B; she is a gift from God in her profession. The depression was dealt with for now, but years later it came back and God taught me how to finally defeat it in my life. Before we venture on the journey, let's take another detour into the future and what God taught me about depression.

****

I am not a doctor and if you are under the care of a doctor, please follow your doctor's orders. If you feel you need to see a doctor, please do not hesitate to seek help. Depression is nothing to fool with. God has given us the gift of doctors and medicines. I will share how God gave me a breakthrough and I pray it helps others suffering with this.

I think I always struggled with slight depression. My life moved at such a fast pace it didn't catch me, but I never suffered from severe depression. That would change. I went through a two-week period where a spirit of heaviness was on me, and for a couple of days I remember it being so bad I was starting to become very concerned about whether I was going to make it through life. It's tough because you feel isolated and trapped in despair. I lost interest in everything, and no matter what I thought about didn't help. I thought of vacation, doing something fun—nothing helped. My mother-in-law lost her sister and I was so depressed I couldn't muster the energy to comfort her. It was a very scary time.

I remember one night I woke up feeling so depressed when I was trying to sleep before work. Earlier in the day I was helping someone that God had put on my heart. As I lay in bed I said to God, "I can't do this anymore. I'm trying to be Your hands and feet, I'm trying to live a life pleasing to You, but I feel this heaviness and I feel under constant attack. I feel like I'm living a defeated Christian walk. I feel someday You will have me share Your goodness, Your faithfulness, and Your love. How can I share that when I am struggling with this depression? I don't believe I should be struggling with this if I truly believe You are who You say You are."

A few moments after laying there in bed, I felt inspired to get serious and start writing this book, to stop talking about it and start doing. I got up from bed, turned the lights on, and that spirit of heaviness lifted as I began to write. In the next few weeks, I wrote nineteen chapters. Later that night I felt God speak to me and say, *"You're right, I didn't design the Christian walk to be lived defeated."*

That same night God led me to listen to a sermon, and the most important ingredient in my breakthrough of depression and feeling like I was constantly under spiritual attack finally sunk in. I heard a sermon on reading and studying God's word daily. Sure, I'd heard it before, but it now really resonated with me. Don't just read it, *study* it. If you miss a day, you're missing the food for your soul. Jeremiah, the prophet, said, *"I eat Your words, Lord."* Job, who suffered more than any human being, said, *"I treasure Your word more than daily bread."*

Once I consistently read and studied God's word daily, I felt like I was standing on solid ground. The Bible says to be transformed by the renewing of our minds. (Romans 12:2): *"Do not conform to the pattern of this world, but be transformed by the renewing of your mind."* We have to get the junk out and replace all that garbage with God's Word. On Christ the solid ground I stand, all other ground is sinking sand. The Bible says, (John 1:14): *"The Word became flesh and dwelt among us, and we behold His glory, the glory as of the only begotten of the Father, full of grace and truth."* His Word becomes part of you. The Apostle Paul tells us in Ephesians Chapter 6: *"Put on the full armor of God and the only part of the armor that is not defensive but offensive to fight back against the Devil is the Sword of the Spirit, which is the Word of God."*

(Isaiah 61:3): *"The garment of praise for the spirit of heaviness."*

If you read that carefully, heaviness/depression is a spirit—a spirit that does not come from God but from Satan. When you feel heaviness/depression come on, a lightbulb should go off that Satan is at your door. Are you going to let him in? The minute I start feeling depressed I'll turn on worship music and even if I don't feel like it, I worship God. I change and redirect my thoughts. I'll cry out to God, "Help, Lord, Help, Lord!" I have noticed that since reading God's Word daily my footing is solid. The Word is your foundation, and you are only as strong as your foundation.

Over these last ten or so years of trying to draw close to God, I realize He was teaching me. As my Heavenly father, He knows my thoughts were robbing me of the joy and peace He has for me. The books He was putting into my hands were correcting my destructive way of thinking. This helped me dramatically. Negative thoughts lead to negative emotions, and negative emotions lead to depression. You must replace those negative thoughts with positive thoughts, and positive thoughts will lead to positive emotions.

(Philippians 4:8): *"Finally, brethren, whatever things are true, whatever things are noble, whatever things are just, whatever things are pure, whatever things are lovely, whatever things are of good report, if there is any virtue and there is anything praiseworthy, meditate on these things."*

If a thought is not going to lift and encourage us, then we need to replace it with one that will. Folks, we are in the midst of a spiritual battle. The Apostle Paul says in (Ephesians 6:12): *"For we do not wrestle against flesh and blood, but against principalities, against powers, against rulers of the darkness of this age, against spiritual hosts of wickedness in the Heavenly places."*

We need to put on the armor of God, which is in Ephesians as well. The sword which is the Word of God is the only part of the armor that attacks back against evil. If you remember when Jesus was brought into the desert and tempted by Satan, He defeated him with the Word of God. Three times he was tempted and all three times he quoted the Word of God to defeat Satan. I truly believe I suffered these bouts of depression and anxiety so that I would have empathy toward those going through it. Depression is horrific and the hopelessness you feel is awful. Anxiety can be so scary. If you have experienced this, you understand what someone going through it feels. I have nothing but compassion, love, and support for these people. Always seek medical help if you struggle with these conditions. We are always to pray for healing and God's wisdom, but stay under the care of medical help until released.

As I close out this chapter, I would like to stress the importance of reading the Word of God daily. The Scriptures will renew your mind, solidify your foundation, and feed your soul. In the next chapter I will talk about Deuteronomy and how Satan tried to snare me, but God's Word protected me.

Let's take that detour and we'll get back on course to the journey.

Chapter Fourteen

The Trap of the Devil

I was at the Knickerbocker Arena in downtown Albany. My friends and I were there for an event. I was getting something to drink and eat and the lady behind the counter said, "You're the Bull."

I said, "What's the Bull?"

She asked me what was the date of my birthday. I told her May 15th. She said, "I knew it, you're Taurus, the Bull."

I said, "Please just give me a drink and popcorn." I went and sat down, but after a moment or two, curiosity was killing me. I got up and now no one was around and I asked her what the Bull and Taurus meant. She went on to describe me to a T.

She said, "You're the nicest guy, but look out when you get mad, you turn into a bull." She said some other stuff too that was accurate but those two traits are what stood out the most.

So, guess what that got Jon doing? You guessed it—reading my horoscope daily, until one day God in His perfect love had me read:

(Deuteronomy 18:10-13): *"One who practices witchcraft, or a soothsayer, or one who interprets omens, or sorcerer, or one who conjures spells, or a medium, or a spiritist, or one who calls up the dead. For all these things are an abomination to the Lord."*

(Deuteronomy 4:19): *"And take heed, lest you lift your eyes to Heaven, and when you see the sun, the moon, and the stars, all the hosts of Heaven, you feel driven to worship them and serve them."*

The conviction of the Holy Spirit was so strong—that reading horoscopes was forbidden by God and an abomination. That is a strong word, but it's a warning that you're playing with fire and it is something God hates. Remember, Jesus quoted the Book of Deuteronomy three times to Satan when he was tempted in the desert, and now these verses in the same powerful book that Jesus quoted were being read by me. You could be walking with God and doing this because you think it's harmless, then wonder why your life is a mess and constantly in turmoil or you have no peace. Jesus did it all, we can have no other gods before Him. This is how incredibly cunning Satan is. He had a nice older lady try and hook me on something that God hates. Remember, Satan studies your life and uses it against you to deceive you.

My sister who was possessed-snared by Satan said that two times he showed himself to her and she was freaked out and scared to death. One of those times she was laying in her bed and my grandmother was rocking in the chair. She said, "Grandma." But she was smart enough to know it couldn't be our grandmother, who had died. She said, "That's not Grandma," and then Satan appeared. I share that because my grandmother's death was what sent my sister over the edge, which drew her to be angry with God and turn to Satan. This shows he studies our lives and will use anything to direct our attention away from God. The Bible says in (1 Peter 5:8): *"Be alert and of sober mind."* Your enemy, Satan, prowls around like a roaring lion, looking for someone to devour. I know some of you think this is small stuff but it is not, you are playing with fire.

So,all the stories you might have been told about a fortune-tellers who give "correct information "are,from what I have learned,in my opinion,Satan studying your life and communicating with that person. God's Word says the gifts of God are irrevocable (Romans 11:29), meaning if God gifted a person in a special way and they don't use that gift for His honor, that person can still access the gift but it is no longer used for glorifying God. I know this stuff can be intriguing,and some of these mediums can justify they are using their words for good and to help people,but these verses from the Bible say it is deception you can't talk with the dead. (Luke 16:26): *"And beside all this, between us and you there is a great gulf fixed: so that they which would pass from hence to you cannot; neither can they pass to us, that would come from thence."* (Job 7:10) is another verse affirming this. These two verses share that there is no communing with the dead.

If we love God, we try our best to honor Him. God forbids fortune-tellers, astrology, and sorcery, etc. If you want God's favor, honor and obey Him. When you walk with God you learn to trust Him, and part of that trust is relying on Him for everything in your life, big and small. He is in all the details. Pray to Him and He will guide you; you don't need to read your horoscope or see a fortune-teller. There are huge spiritual and life consequences from this. Ask God your innermost questions, He will answer you in ways you never imagined. He wants to be Lord of your life. As for that "bull" temper, I was set free from it in Jesus, and as long as I spend time with God, it is only a part of my past. Love is patient, love has self-control, these are fruits of the spirit. Praise God!

Let's get back to the journey. I have some moving stories of God's love to share.

Chapter Fifteen

On Fire

Even as a little boy, I always had a heart for God and a love for Him. Yes, I was a little rascal doing all the things I shouldn't do, but the foundation was there. Dragging us kids to church finally worked. My mom would always tell me she dedicated me to God from the womb. My mom always shared that she was told she couldn't have any more children due to complications from the prior four pregnancies, but then she became pregnant with me. She called me the miracle baby and one night had a beautiful experience she felt was the Holy Spirit, and told God if it was a boy she would name him Jon, after John the Baptist. Back then you couldn't tell the gender of the child until the child was born. Was it because of that story that I always felt a purpose to my life, a calling for God? Was it because she shared that in my impressionable years and it programmed me? And if God really did have a purpose for me, why had I lived such a sinful life?

God has a purpose for everyone's life and as you draw closer to Him you will find your unique calling. I love that God has no favorites, He loves us all equally. Yes, He gifts and uses others in more powerful ways but He loves us equally! Please understand that.

(Romans 2:11): *"God has no favorites."*

(Ephesians 6:9): *"Masters, do the same to them, and stop your threat, knowing that He who is both their Master and yours is in Heaven, and that there is no partiality with Him."*

God loved Billy Graham the same way He loves you. Yes, he gifted and anointed him in a more powerful way, but He loves us the same.

Because of the impact of my mom dedicating me from the womb to the Lord, I dedicated all three of my children and my two granddaughters while they were in the womb. I suggest all that are pregnant or become pregnant seriously think about doing that. What a difference it would make in this world. If your child is already born, then dedicate and pray for them now.

I love what A.W. Tozer, a theologian that was used powerfully by God, said: "We are only as close to God as we choose to be."

(Jeremiah 29:13): *"You will seek Me and find Me when you seek Me with all your heart."*

I finally felt as close to God again as I did when I surrendered my life to Him at fourteen. I longed to be back at peace with the Lord. I was on fire for God and He was moving in such a powerful way showing me He really does know each of us intimately.

(Matthew 10:30): *"And the very hairs on your head are numbered."* God backs this verse up with science, as you read in an earlier chapter explaining how our DNA has a special code that not one other person in the entire world has. *You are sealed by God!* Take your fingerprint, toe print, tongue print—no one has *your* print. God's signature is all over you! If there wasn't a designer, our blood wouldn't have a code. God designed you in your mother's womb (Psalms 139). Take the time to read that psalm. God loves you more than you could ever comprehend. You are written on the palm of His hand.

****

On July 12, 2014, I was baptized at Grace Fellowship Church. It was such a meaningful, special day! It took me forty-one years to get into that water and surrender my life fully to Jesus Christ, my Lord and Savior. I'm so proud to say that! I love what Baptism symbolizes. I went into that water with all my sin and shame and came out of that water with my sin and shame washed away. I have a new beginning. I am a child of God. I ran from God for most of my life except for those few years I surrendered to Him at fourteen years old.

We all have that stereotypical way of thinking that God wants to rob us of our joy and send us on "the mission field in some remote place." Where did we ever get that way of thinking? I'll bet Satan is behind it. The exact opposite is true. God's plan and purpose for your life is perfect. (Romans 12:2) Then you will be able to test and approve God's will is—His good, pleasing and perfect will. It is where you find joy. He created you and knows exactly what you need and what completes you. Look at a rose, how beautiful it is. Look at the beach, the ocean. Look at the sun rising or a picturesque sunset. Look at nature, a little baby with all its fingers and toes, so perfect. God doesn't do anything without putting His signature on it. Everything He does is creative and perfect, including you. No one else can do what you were called and created to do for Him.

Prior to my Baptism, God opened my eyes with books, sermons, and my alone time with Him. As I shared earlier, I never read a book till I was in my mid to late thirties. Now, I love to read, and God spoke clearly to me through the books He brought into my life. God speaks to us in so many ways—through people, sermons, music, dreams, visions, and a still small voice. The Bible also says angels can minister to us.

(Hebrews 13:2): *"Do not forget to show hospitality to strangers, for by doing so some people have shown hospitality to angels without knowing it."*

I have found that God speaks to us differently as individuals. Most of the time God puts an impression on my heart and it doesn't go away, it just keeps coming back until I do what He is prompting me to do. I have heard the voice of God speak to me internally. There's a heightened silence and then He speaks. Every time God has spoken to me I have been alone with Him, except for one time, at a funeral service. We were celebrating the life of a very special young man named Ernie DuPont. I remember the presence of God being so strong at this service. Many of the people who cared for him and knew him during his struggle shared the impact Ernie had on them. Our oldest daughter Devyn went to grade school with Ernie at Our Savior's Lutheran School till we moved and enrolled her in public school. Ernie had a heart for God and later would teach at Vacation Bible School at OSL which our two youngest kids would attend. Sadly, Ernie succumbed to a very rare disease called Degos Disease. While I was in the presence of other people celebrating this young man's life of significance, God spoke to me twice at that service. The first thing God spoke to me was a question. He said, *"Jon, do you want to live a life of significance or make a lot of money?"* I remember I had to think for a moment, and I answered, "I want to live a life of significance, but I need You to help me." God was comparing significance to this young man's life. The reason I had to think on it was I knew the way I was driven and I knew my weaknesses. Absolutely, I wanted to live a life of significance, but I needed God's help to do that.

I had plans when I retired from my full-time job of possibly creating a blacktop business, a tree-cutting business, expanding the landscaping business, and even thought about going back into the restaurant business. The second thing God said to me later at that service was, *"I want you to pitch a tent for me."* I was floored. The significance behind what God just said to me had so much meaning. Every time I would do a landscaping job and someone needed the job done for a prom or a wedding, etc., I would say, "I don't care what it takes to get this job done, if I have to, I will pitch a tent for you," meaning, I would get it done no matter what. God was saying He wanted me to be committed to Him with the same vigor I committed to my customers.

I realized that God does hear every word we speak. That is amazing but convicting. We have to guard our tongues, and if it is not pleasing to God, don't say it. Think about that. God says He hears every word we speak and He showed me He does. I remember the Holy Spirit impressing on my heart to stay in the Book of James for a month, reading and meditating on it over and over. I would write myself notes on controlling my tongue and remind myself not to speak unless my words were pleasing to God. When we remember that God hears every word we say, it helps us to be conscious of what we speak. I was also praying to become a better listener. We don't want to miss what God is trying to communicate with us.

(John 10:27): *"My sheep hear My voice, and I know them, and they follow Me."*

Jesus calls your alone time with God, the secret place.

(Matthew 6:6): *"But when you pray, go into your room, close the door, and pray to your Father, who is unseen."*

I think my alone time with God is where I have drawn the closest to Him. All spiritual disciplines draw you closer to God. On this journey there have been times God's presence has been very strong. Then, there have been many times when I wondered where God was.

We can't base our walk with God on just feelings and emotions. You must hold onto those times God has shown you He is there.

Writing this book has helped me relive those special moments God has given me. It is faith knowing He is there and hears every word I pray.

(Hebrews 11:6): *"And without faith it is impossible to please God."*

We sometimes think God was holding Abraham's hand the whole time, or Mary's, Joseph's, Peter's, the Apostle Paul's. He was not. Just like with you or me, He would guide them and then their faith would "kick in." I love the verse in James 5:17. Elijah was a human as we are, and yet when he prayed earnestly that no rain would fall, none fell for three and a half years! Elijah, a man used powerfully by God, is just like you or me. The more time you spend with Him and the longer you walk with Him, the more you trust Him. God is so faithful! I will share in a later chapter a few pivotal paradigm shifts God was guiding and redirecting me toward, through books.

Before we close out this chapter, I want to leave you with the websites to see Ernie Dupont discuss his battle with Degos Disease (Fighting Degos Disease) Youtube.com. Anyone feeling moved to donate in honor of Ernie Dupont to help fight the disease for others, that site is: www.Steffens-scleroderma.org.

The definition of significance is "the quality of being worthy of attention; importance." My definition of significance would add to that with this: "In spite of your circumstances, your situation, your pain, fear, and when you do not understand, you still exalt the name of Jesus and glorify Him." Think about that. When God references significance to you, you have finished this race well! I know Ernie's parents and family are so proud of him and so am I!

For now, though, let's journey on to January of 2015, my first Mission trip.

Chapter Sixteen

Guatemala Mission Trip

Everyone should experience a Mission trip at some point. You say to God on your Mission, "God, here I am, what do You want to teach me? I want to be Your hands and feet with no distractions."

It wakes you up to realize how blessed we are and all we take for granted without ever really having a heart of gratitude for the little things, which are really big things. I think it's a perfect opportunity to take a leap of faith. By the end of the Mission, you'll be closer to God and more loving and compassionate at home. It moves you.

In January 2015, I embarked on my Mission trip to Guatemala. We missed our plane out of Miami and our jumper plane into the jungle out of Guatemala City. It was Monday night and I was wondering, since it took 2 ½ to 3 days to get there, why would God allow this time to be wasted? We didn't get a chance to interact with the kids that day, but we did get a chance to start our project for the jungle school. I was feeling stressed at not being able to talk with our youngest daughter Jillian who was having a hard time not communicating with us. Also, I wasn't feeling God's presence and was wrestling with a few things. I knew I had to get up early and spend time with God.

I had very high expectations for this trip, not that I was putting the Lord God to the test. I knew we had to be there for a reason. I felt if the rest of the trip was like this my faith would be crushed. We can't base our walk on feelings but on faith—the things we can't see and touch. But I knew in my spirit this trip would bring me closer to God. I knew my attitude was wrong and I needed to cry out to God.

Tuesday morning, I got up at 5:30 a.m. and went out to the pavilion to pray. I read the 40th Psalm which says God will not forsake us, He will rescue us against the pits and the attacks of Satan and overwhelm us with His love and presence. I prayed and said, "Lord, this is my prayer." That morning one of the leaders and another gentleman came out and we started talking. I shared part of my testimony and started to feel a little better like I was climbing out of the pit. (Revelation 12:11): *"They conquered by the word of their testimony."* When we share our testimony, our faith is strongest.

At 7:00 a.m., we greeted the children, who were so affectionate, appreciative, and loving. Shortly after, a few of us went to one of the children's classes. They began their day with prayer in Spanish, which was extremely moving to see. Suddenly, I noticed tears streaming down my cheeks. I looked over at Matt and he was also wiping tears from his cheeks. We knew we were in the presence of the Holy Spirit. As I write this, it brings me back to that special moment knowing we were in the presence of God. It was awesome to see people praising God in another language, and I could already feel God answering my prayer.

We headed over to breakfast. As I was in the line, the song "Holy, Holy, Holy" in Spanish was playing and the Holy Spirit came on me like a flood. I walked out, not wanting to be seen full of emotion, to the pavilion where less than three hours ago I cried out to God to pull me from the pit and overwhelm me with His presence. It was ironic that I was overfilled with His love and joy of the spirit in the same spot where I prayed to God for help. God did not forsake me. I just praised Him and thanked Him for His love and for being so faithful. From this point on, my faith was strengthened.

We worked all day Tuesday on projects and got to know each other. On Wednesday, our first stop was to one of the homes of a student who lived with her aunt. It was incredible to see—there were dirt floors and you could see through the walls. There were hammocks and a little mattress to sleep on, no running water, and an outhouse to use for a bathroom. Hard to fathom. We gathered around and our leader Warren prayed a blessing, and as he did I was overwhelmed with compassion for these people. I felt shame for all the times I didn't have a heart of gratitude for the many blessings I had back home. These people have so little but seemed so content and grateful. We gave them a blessing bag we had made and visited with their neighbor across the street. JonMichael, my son, gave some Beanie Babies, donations from Grace Fellowship that we brought from home, to this beautiful little girl. The little girl's eyes lit up, and we took a picture which is worth a thousand words—it captured a precious moment.

As we got on the bus to travel to the landfill, the mood was somber, and one of the guys made a poignant statement, "Who's to say these people have it wrong?" He was right, we as Americans have it wrong, starting with me first. We get so caught up in stuff or busyness. I just wished their living conditions were better with secure housing, running water, and a little more to live on.

We then went and visited another child from the jungle school. Her house was a replica of what we had just seen. The mother lost her husband to a heart attack and they had two families living together to survive. We gave them a blessing bag and prayed with them also. From there we traveled to the landfill.

We arrived at the landfill to find about ten people there. The regulars know when the city dump trucks came in and that's when the landfill is busier. As we looked around, we saw people picking through the garbage; this was their way of life. This was so sad to see but it was also sad to see the desperation of the animals. We walked around and saw dogs with broken legs, and the sight we were not prepared for was a malnourished dog with a broken back dragging his leg. I couldn't keep looking and had to walk back to the bus. I just wish I had the means to put that poor animal out of its suffering and misery. I later was told by a friend that there was another dog worse off than that one, and the birds and animals were eating it while it was still alive. I am so thankful I didn't have to see that. In this world we have the means to stop this heartache and poverty. The main causes are greed, selfishness, and corruption. Love of God, kindness, and generosity will stop this dead in its tracks.

We all gathered around with the people in the landfill. Some were workers and some were going through the garbage. Anna, our interpreter and guide, who was also a leader at the jungle school, shared that the people wanted us to know that even though their situation was bad they gave God thanks for His many blessings. I will always remember that day. I was moved and felt led to pray for these people and for our Mission team. We felt awful and wished we could heal their poverty, but we also felt our contribution was too small. But if we all do a little, it helps a lot. We then gave them blessing bags and I shook hands with each of them and gave them a pat on the arm. I wanted them to know I wasn't afraid to touch them, and at the foot of the Cross we are all equal. I had Anna tell them we will pray that God blesses them and Jesus loves them. Just then one of the guys picking garbage in the landfill raised his blessing bag toward Heaven and said, "Thank you, Jesus!" I will never forget that man. We were thankful that the landfill wasn't too busy because it would have broken our hearts to not give everyone a blessing bag.

We traveled a very somber ride from there to the Mayan Ruins. You could hear a pin drop, as everyone was full of emotions and caught up in their thoughts. The Mayan Ruins were incredible the way they built the huge cement structures, especially so long ago without modern technology and equipment. We saw where they sacrificed humans to their gods.

We then traveled into a little town to visit some gift shops. While we were there we were approached by four to five children selling key chain trinkets for 15 quetzals. We purchased one from each of them and gave them a little extra. In American money this is so little, it's not even worth talking about. There was an ice cream store, so we bought them each some ice cream. We spent the better part of an hour there and really got to know the kids. Anna had sandwiches left over from the jungle school that we gave to the kids and they were so thankful. A challenged and partially disfigured child walked up and we purchased a key chain from him. One of our leaders, Kathy, felt led earlier to hold a blessing bag for some reason and this kid was the reason—that's often how God works, you just feel led to do something. She gave him the blessing bag and he was thankful and walked away blessed.

As we said goodbye, two little girls approached my son and I, and gave us each a key chain as a gift. My son and I were so moved by this. Here were poor kids giving us a gift because we touched their lives, but really they blessed *us* more then they will ever know. JonMichael and I were about four seats apart on the bus but we looked at each other with smiles ear to ear. It was a joyful, special moment.

The children held a demonstration on our final day at the jungle school. They greeted us and thanked us for coming. We should have been the ones thanking them. I don't think they knew how much they touched our lives with their grateful, loving spirits. They did an amazing job and were so talented. The final night they threw us a special dinner and we shared how we had been touched by this experience. We prayed and sang songs together.

We were on the plane back to the United States and my friend Tom was sitting by the window and noticed there was a halo with the shadow of the plane in it following us. I know the Weather Channel says this happens when the sun aligns with earth but to me it symbolized God sending His guardian angels to watch over us. The next plane out of Miami would be taken out of service because one of the engine's oil pumps broke just before we hit the runway. The pilot told us that had never happened in his thirty years of flying, and it wouldn't have been good if it happened in the air. I knew God was watching over us.

The Mission trip was everything and more. We are looking forward to our team meeting and keeping our friendship and experience alive— to commit to serve here in the States and bring honor and glory to our loving, faithful God.

Chapter Seventeen

Dreams and Visions

When I spend time with God I like to be alone with no distractions. I like my privacy; I don't want anyone listening to me praying. Sometimes we can be praying for very private things or personal struggles. We might want our prayers for others and their situations private. So, at this point in my life, I would go and sit in my truck in an empty parking lot. I'd grab a coffee and listen to a sermon on my Turning Point app with Dr. Jeremiah. Then I would read my Bible and pray.

I kept having the same visions. One was of me sitting alone and some little children, between four and eight years old, who came over and hugged me. They could feel the love of Jesus coming through me, which is what attracted them to me. The second vision was of me preaching. Sometimes it was inside a church and then a couple of times it seemed to be in a stadium with a very big crowd. The third vision was of me writing a book, but also the *desire* to write one.

The first vision I could comprehend because I have always had a heart for children. I love kids, especially when they are young, before they turn into "monsters" (trying to be real here). I feel this vision has already been fulfilled. During the Mission trip the kids at the school would get off the bus and come hug us. One day I had two or three kids hugging me.

The second vision didn't make sense because public speaking scares me to death. At that point I had never spoken publicly. God kept reminding me of a time when I was a young child and sold popcorn and peanuts at the Heritage Baseball Park. The first time I went up into the bleachers to sell popcorn and peanuts I looked at the crowd and walked back down to the office and told them I couldn't do it because I was scared to death! I had to yell, "Popcorn and peanuts here!" It took me three times to finally be able to get the courage to do it. God was using this experience to show me I could conquer my fear. It is through God that you can do what He calls you to do.

(2 Corinthians 12:8-10): *"My grace is sufficient for you, for My strength is made perfect in weakness."*

The third vision was to write a book. God started to make it a desire in my heart, a dream. Since I had never read a book till my mid-thirties and I hated school, I thought, *Lord, you got the wrong guy.* I didn't even know I had the ability to write. So, on that day I prayed, "Lord, are these my visions and dreams or are they Yours? Because if they are mine, just make them go away. If they are Yours, will they ever come to fruition?" That was my exact prayer. This was either Thursday or Friday prior to the Sunday service at Grace Fellowship where God answered that prayer.

Kim and I normally go to the Saturday night service but this week she couldn't go so I went to the Sunday 11:00 a.m. service by myself. The title of the two-part series of the sermon was, "If you are going to be used by God, you have to have dreams, visions, and goals." I almost fell out of the chair. The title of the sermon and everything Pastor Rex was preaching was God speaking directly to me. Then at the end of the sermon he said, "And some of you don't think so but with God you can write a bestselling book." I was floored! I talked to my friend Nick and he went to the 9:00 a.m. service and heard nothing about the bestselling book. I got a CD from the Saturday night service and there was nothing in there about a bestselling book. When I drove home that day I pulled over, sat there, and was undone. I thought, *God, you really do know me. You really do hear my prayers.* The sermon was the first confirmation. God confirmed the book two other ways to me, which with the sermon made three confirmations.

I had an employee who was a recovering heroin addict. At this point in my life, I didn't want to be around a person who struggled with addiction because of the struggles with my sister. I learned drug addicts will steal from anyone to get their next high, so I had a slight phobia of being that close to someone with addiction. I planned to dismiss him in a nice way, but God spoke to my heart and said, *"I want you to keep him."* So, I did. One day he and I were working and I asked him what his parents did for work. He said his father did odd jobs, but his mother for thirty years watched children out of her home but had just recently published two books. Instantly a lightbulb went off and God was saying, *"You see, you can write a book."* This employee and I became friends. He occasionally contacts me even now, and I am so proud of him for pulling himself out of the hole he was in and living a productive life.

The next confirmation was when I was reading a magazine article in the doctor's office about a mother who stayed home to raise her children and published a book. It was God speaking to me again saying, *"You can do it."* When God uses a situation to speak to you, it is heightened and you know He is speaking to you. It's called an *ah ha* moment. One day I was at a men's breakfast and at the end we were talking and suddenly this man with a gift of prophecy pointed at me and full of energy said, "God has called you to preach and you don't understand how He's going to do it but He will do it!" He also said things about my children and that all they were going through was part of the process of getting me there. I was in shock. In this prophecy he said things only my wife, children, and parents knew, but then said something only God knew. Wow!

These visions and dreams are from God. You realize how personally God knows us—every facet of our lives. The Creator of Heaven and Earth, Creator of everything, knows *me*. Unbelievable! Remember, I am a very skeptical person, but when someone prophesizes things only your family and God know, you believe it. I am no longer a skeptic. That's the only confirmation I have had so far for preaching. I have only spoken publicly giving eulogies and my testimony. I am in no hurry. That could be many years away, and I might only speak a time or two. I don't try to analyze it anymore, it will drive me crazy trying to figure out how and when it will happen. Sometimes we just want God to tell us, but there's something so special and overwhelming when God puts something on your heart and then brings it to fruition in His special way.

Remember, it is faith that pleases God. God has visions for you as well but you need to draw close to Him. When you spend time alone with God regularly, Jesus calls it the secret place (Matthew 6:6), you really see the heart of God. I feel I have drawn so much closer in my alone time with Him. Remember, it is relationship, not religion. God has shown me my joy is in Him and being used by Him.

Let's journey on to two very special, divine moments.

Chapter Eighteen

Joy—An Amazing Day for Both of Us!

I received a call from Mr. Rueckert, a member of my childhood church and a customer of mine. He let me know that his next-door neighbor was dying of cancer and that he and his wife wanted to pay me to do a cleanup for their house. An act of love. I let them know that I would take care of it. I started praying for her healing and interceding for her before God. I have always had a heart for those who are sick. I always pray for their healing and their comfort, and that they accept Jesus Christ as their Lord and Savior before they die. The time came for me to do both cleanups and I remember it was a hot spring day, but a beautiful day. At this point in my business, I had four to five employees. When I work I wear headphones that play music and I listen to K-Love or Air-1—both Christian music stations—all day long. The guys will laugh at me at times because occasionally I will sing out loud and when the equipment stops running they can hear me. Let's just say I can't make singing my day job.

I didn't journal at this time in my life consistently, but I was praying for her while we worked on her lawn. We finished the lawn and as the guys were packing the equipment away I saw the Johnsons, friends of my parents and members of my childhood church, come out of the house. As they walked down the driveway with somber looks, I approached them and asked how she was doing and if she knew the Lord. They replied, "She is very sick." They shook their heads. "Sadly, she doesn't know the Lord and doesn't want to talk about God at all." I said, "We'll have to keep her in prayer." I walked back and got in the truck and I felt the Lord speak to me, *"I want you to go speak to her."* I thought to myself, *Are you kidding me, Lord? You just heard them say she doesn't want anything to do with talking about God.* I don't like pushing my faith on people, that's not how it works, but I knew God was speaking to me. His presence was strong.

Sometimes God gives us gentle nudging and sometimes He gives very strong signals. I knew if I didn't go it would be disobedient and I would regret it. It was more than a gentle prompting. So, I bowed my head and prayed. I said, "Lord, I'll go but I need you to give me the words to say."

I jumped out of the truck and quickly reached back in and grabbed a business card off the dashboard. As I walked to the front door, I was stressed thinking about what the Johnsons just told me—*"She wants nothing to do with talking about God."* I rang the bell and a very tall man came to the door. It was a screen door and he looked through at me in a very serious state, which added to the anxiousness I was already feeling. I said, "The Rueckerts paid for me to do your cleanup but here is my business card. I know your situation and if there is anything I can do to help, please don't hesitate to call, it's free of charge. I don't care what it is—hedges, mowing the lawn, even moving furniture around, please don't hesitate to call, I would love to help you." As I looked in, I saw a frail woman wrapped in a blanket with oxygen in her nose. You could tell she was in the end stage of her disease. She was so weak, but she slowly lifted her two fingers to motion me to come in.

Her husband saw that she wanted me to come in, so he opened the door without saying a word. I walked in and talked with them for about twenty minutes. They listened to every word I said, but I do not remember anything I said to them, as I believe the Holy Spirit was speaking through me. The only thing I do remember was sharing with her about how God showed me that my brother who passed away in 1985 was with Him. His story is worth repeating.

I struggled wondering if my brother was with the Lord because he hadn't really lived the way he should, but God gave me the poignant memory of when my brother was kicked out of the house as a young adult. He came home for dinner one night and when he was leaving, my mom grabbed him by the jacket, pulled him in, and said, "Jimmy, if you died tonight, do you know where you would go?" My brother said, "Yes, Mom, I would go to Heaven." My mom pulled him in by his big puffy jacket and said, "Why?" My brother said, "Because I believe in Jesus Christ as my Lord and Savior." Eternal life with God is a gift, we can't earn it.

(John 3:16): *"For God so loved the world that He gave His only begotten son, that whosoever believes in Him shall not perish but have eternal life."*

Don't stop there, though, read the next verse:

(John 3:17) *"For God did not send His Son into the world to condemn it but to save it."*

So many of you need to hear that. *Jesus is God's greatest act of love to humankind.*

When I finished talking with them I said, "You have my business card, I don't care whatever you need I will help you free of charge, please don't hesitate to call." I finished with, "All I want to do is make your day."

As I turned and walked toward the door in a faint voice, the woman said, "Jon…" When I turned around she said with a smile on her face, "You just did!"

I knew she got it! She now understood who Jesus was. I also believe her husband understood, because he just looked at me, soaking in every word God spoke through me. As I walked to my truck I felt such joy. I was just used by God, and it was one of the most amazing times of my life. The joy you feel when you are obedient and can sense God's pleasure in you is indescribable. My wife and I were on vacation and having a wonderful time. As I looked out over the bay to the right and the ocean to the left, referring back to this special divine moment, I said, "I will remember that special day till I die." Not only was I used by God, but the only thing I remember sharing was the poignant memory about my brother. That made the day even more special.

Six months later, the Rueckerts invited us to sit at their table for a Youth for Christ gathering. At the end of the gathering, Mr. Rueckert pulled up a chair and said, "I don't know what you said to her but someone we know (I believe it might have been the woman's daughter) believes she came to know the Lord before she died." It confirmed everything I felt that day and meant the world to me. I also believe her husband is with the Lord also as he died shortly after her. One day when I get to Heaven I believe I will see them there.

The following poem by Corrie ten Boom comes to mind when I think of Mr. Rueckert's neighbor:

> *"When I enter that beautiful city, and the saints all around me appear, I hope that someone will tell me: it was you who invited me here."*

There are two points I want you, the reader, to come away with from this story. One, is that this dying woman was probably in her mid-to-late seventies and for some reason was completely turned off to God. This could have been true her entire life, or maybe it was midstream, we don't know. Whatever the reason, she wanted nothing to do with God, even on her deathbed, but that's where God's amazing love comes in. He sets into motion a caring neighbor—a landscaper—to give this woman one more chance to receive His love and spend eternity with Him. I am so glad she opened her heart to receive that love. That is the God I pray you come to know by the end of this book, from the most unlikely person to write one.

Second, your joy is in the Lord. God was giving me so many *ah ha* moments and showing me my love for Him and service to Him was where my joy was. There's no better feeling than helping someone in need. As you draw close to God, He will draw even closer to you and show you He created you and knows you better than you know yourself. He has an amazing journey for you! If you have never invited Jesus into your heart, please take the time right now to do that: *Father God, I come before you and confess my sin and that I am a sinner, I believe in Jesus, Your son, and invite Him to be Lord and Savior of my life. Please help me to walk out this journey with You.*

Then buckle your seat belt and hold on because you're going for an exciting ride, a ride you can't even fathom or imagine.

Let's journey on to another *ah ha* moment of joy.

Chapter Nineteen

Another Joyful Experience — Hearing Powerful Words

It was June 7th and Kim's uncle was in serious shape. His blood pressure was 60/20. He fights anxiety and depression. I had a long day at work and just wanted to get a good jumpstart on the day and get as much done as I could. Hedges can be back-breaking and this was a big job. I brought a shirt to change into at lunchtime so I could freshen up and then go visit her uncle. As I was traveling to the jobsite, the Lord was prompting me to go see her uncle now before I started working. The prompting was strong and I knew if I didn't go it would be disobedience. I had all my equipment and my dump trailer so I called my good friend Nick and asked if I could park my truck and trailer at his house and use his car to go to Albany Medical Center. He said yes.

I got to Albany Medical Center and as I walked from the parking garage to the building to visit Kim's uncle, I passed a man who was very distraught and upset. I heard him tell the person on the other end of the phone that she was in a coma. I felt like I should ask him if he wanted me to pray with him, that's how distraught he was, but the prompting wasn't strong enough for me to ask him.

I went up to Kim's uncle's room on the 6th floor in ICU and her uncle said, "I was waiting for you." He said he knew I was going to come down and visit. That meant a lot to me—God must have put that on his heart, or a sense that he was sending someone. Sometimes we don't think our lives make a difference, but they do. I shared what I felt the Lord had put on my heart for him. I told her uncle I felt the Lord wants him to know He knows his pain, and He is there for him. I shared that he must read God's word regularly and memorize a few Scriptures to combat Satan.

(2 Timothy 1:7): *"For God has not given us a spirit of fear, but of power and of love and of a sound mind."*

(Proverbs 12:25): *"Anxiety in the heart of man causes depression."*

It was a very nice visit and I think we both felt God's presence. I prayed with Kim's uncle and left him a Bible to read. I was with her uncle for about forty-five minutes. After visiting him on the 6th floor, the ICU floor, I went to the elevator and the distraught man I saw on the way in was now waiting for the elevator on the same floor. He was on the phone again. I knew God wanted me to speak to him now; it was a divine moment. I said, "Excuse me, would you like me to pray with you?" He looked at me in shock, then looked at the phone, then looked back at me and said, "Hold on." He then told the person on the other end of the phone he would call him back. I said, "I heard you talking about someone you love who is in a coma." He told me his name was Jason and said, "Yes, my girlfriend Anna. She has seizures and collapsed on our front lawn." I think he said he had to perform CPR on her. He said a pastor stopped by and helped them get to the hospital. Not sure if he called an ambulance or drove them. I didn't ask. He said, "I've never thought about God before and here a pastor helps us and then you ask to pray with me." Just then the elevator doors opened and he invited me in and hit the button for the main floor. I asked if it was okay for me to pray for him. He said yes. I laid a hand on his left shoulder and began to pray for everything the Holy Spirit was putting on my heart. I prayed for healing for Anna and that God's presence would be felt in the room, that he would appoint guardian angels to stand by her bedside, and that he would comfort Jason.

As I was praying I was also having a side conversation with God. It was a Friday and the hospital was extremely busy that day and I'm not bold, I'm very private in many ways, but I knew God brought us together and that's nothing to take lightly. I prayed to God, "I know this is a divine moment and I am here to do what You called me to do, I don't care if that door opens and people are looking at us, I will pray what You want me to pray." Remember, as I am having this side conversation with God, I am still praying over Jason. I felt the elevator land on the main floor and as I was praying I was waiting for the doors to open. The elevator sat on the floor for a while as I kept praying. I knew it was God keeping the elevator shut, I had no doubt at all. Suddenly, as if Jesus himself were standing right behind me and spoke in my right ear, I heard, *Pray that Jason and Anna come to know Jesus Christ as their Lord and Savior."* I repeated what I heard and then said, "In the name of Jesus, Amen." Just then the doors of the elevator opened. Jason jumped back in awe and with great excitement said, "Did you notice that the whole time you were praying and praying and praying, the elevator doors stayed shut and when you were finished praying they opened?" I said, "Jason, you were just in the presence of God, that was the Holy Spirit."

Jason gave me a big bear hug and was lifting me up, he was so excited. We were both in the presence of God. Absolutely amazing, and what a privilege! I was so pumped up and full of joy for the Lord that as I turned and walked away I saw three men and almost grabbed them and said, "Do you know Jesus?" I was so full of joy and happiness; I couldn't contain it. God was showing me that my joy and happiness was in Him. After I left the hospital, I put Jason and Anna on two church prayer chains. I still pray for them today and maybe one day our paths will cross. Your joy and happiness comes from the Lord as well!

As I shared, it was as if Jesus himself spoke into my right ear, *"Pray that Jason and Anna come to know Jesus Christ as their Lord and Savior."* The Holy Spirit just said it, why do *I* have to say it? I have to say it because I am human and it brings the Heavenly realm down to the earthly realm. Now, God is involved and the victory is His. Our job is to pray and activate the spiritual realm. There is incredible power in prayer. If we could only comprehend it, we would pray more.

When Kim's uncle was released from the hospital, Kim's mom Jane shared that he was in the bathroom shaving, taking care of himself and singing. He was happy and doing well. Why? Because he was just fed and I gave him a Bible which is the Word of God, the Sword of the Spirit, our weapon to fight off Satan. Through our conversation, he knew that God loved him—he got it. The Sword is our weapon to battle the enemy, to battle the negative thoughts that Satan tries to put there. Unfortunately, Kim's uncle soon fell back into defeat and the depression and anxiety are consuming his joy. I can't stress enough that you must read the Bible daily and spend time with God, even just ten to fifteen minutes to start. The more you do it, the more you will get to know God. The Bible says the Devil roars around like a lion seeking whom he can devour (1 Peter 5:8). You are no match for Satan unless you put on God's armor and use your sword, then you'll be victorious (Ephesians 6). God allowed me to see into the spiritual realm. *We are in a battle!*

Before we journey on, let's take a quick detour and I'll share how God helped me with anxiety.

Chapter Twenty

Anxiety Detour

A s I have shared through this journey, God has helped me with negative thinking patterns and depression. He has also helped me with anxiety. Because of my childhood I would go through life and feel that if I didn't worry about something happening, then it would happen. I thought that if I *did* worry about it, that would possibly prevent it from happening. I look back at this now and realize how completely wrong this way of thinking is. (Matthew 6:34*): "Therefore, do not worry about tomorrow, for tomorrow will worry about itself. Each day has enough trouble of its own."* When we learn to get to know God by spending time with Him—relationship not religion—we learn to trust Him. Worrying will not change anything. The only thing worry does is rob us of our peace and joy. Worry is inconsistent (Matthew 6:25). Worry is irrational (Matthew 6:26). Worry is ineffective (Matthew 6:27). Worry is illogical (Matthew 6:28-30). Worry is irreligious (Matthew 6:31,32). (*Jeremiah Study Bible*, page 1292).

I thank God I am free from this sickness. I'm not saying I never worry but when I start, I go right to God and give the concern to Him. Also, as I look back I see that God has walked with me through everything, no matter what. I pray against the bad possibilities, but I have come to know God more intimately and know He will never leave or forsake me, and He has always been there for me and with me (Hebrews 13:5). Worry, anxiety, and depression, in my opinion, are all linked.

My anxiety started from a bad experience in the dental chair. I was having an old filling replaced and the dentist had a dental dam set up in my mouth. A dental dam is like an umbrella they put inside your mouth—they cut a hole in it so you can breathe, and this stops anything from falling down your throat. I think this helps the dentist see more clearly the area he is working on. Well, with the chair in the downward position and the dam in my mouth, I was drowning in saliva and the hygienist wasn't sucking it out properly so I felt like I was choking. Panic came over me so I asked the dentist to take everything out of my mouth so I could pull myself together. Prior to this, I never had anxiety at the dentist. I made it through that visit, but then every time I went to the dentist after that incident, I had anxiety and it didn't stop there. I started getting anxious at the eye doctor as well. I was starting to notice that my anxiety was growing. During this time, I had my first and thankfully my only panic attack; an absolutely terrible experience and those who have had one understand what I'm talking about. A panic attack is like a living Hell. I felt God was putting on my heart that if I didn't deal with this, it would control me. This is how people get to the point of not leaving their house and become crippled with fear.

I went to prayer. One of the verses I learned to memorize was (2 Timothy 1:7): *"For God hasn't given you a spirit of fear but of power, love, and a sound mind."* When you look closely at this, fear is a spirit—a spirit that does not come from God. It comes from Satan. And what is Satan's job? To torment, rob you of your peace and joy, and ultimately pull you completely away from God. So, the first thing I recognized was that this false fear doesn't come from God, it comes from Satan. God will give you a sound mind, which means *peaceful* mind. Every time I felt anxious I would repeat this verse (sometimes twenty times). The other thing I would do was wear iPods and listen to Christian worship music. Satan hates worship. The worship music would remind me who my God is and that He is with me. If Satan is trying to torment you, run to God and Satan will flee. Satan doesn't want to do anything that pushes you towards God. So, I run to God. If I feel anxiety coming on, instantly I am repeating (2 Timothy 1:7) and I listen to worship music, open the Bible and read, or listen to a sermon. I stay as close to God as I can, I put on the armor of God daily (Ephesians 6). The Word of God is your foundation and your weapon against the enemy. Soak it in. (Romans 12:12) When you read God's Word it renews your mind. (Proverbs 23:7) *"As a man thinketh, so is he."*

If we are going to think in destructive ways it will cause destruction. The Bible renews your mind and teaches you how to reboot and think correctly. I suggest reading *As a Man Thinketh,* by James Allen. This book shows us the power of our minds. We should learn to control our thoughts, not let our thoughts control us. Another book that God brought into my hands is *The Power of Positive Thinking,* by Norman Vincent Peale, which focuses on how to view life and problems through a Christian aspect. When you put your hand into God's, He will guide you. God communicates with you in many ways. He will use books, sermons, people, music, visions, dreams, an impression on your heart, possibly an angel, and by a still small voice. God communicates with you in the way He knows you will best receive it. As you look back on your life, you might see things you missed in the moment but now realize it was God guiding you.

Before we close this detour, I want to stress that if you struggle with anxiety or depression, seek a medically certified counselor. This is nothing to be ashamed of. Some of you have had horrific experiences and have been through a lot. There are many things that can cause anxiety and depression, and a certified counselor can help you with this. I know well-renowned people who see counselors regularly. I have in the past and would not hesitate at all if I felt I needed to again. Life can be overwhelming so consulting a professional can help us to handle our thoughts and feelings and to deal with them in a positive way. God has given us the gift of doctors and medicines if needed.

Remember, it is relationship, not religion, and it takes spending time with God to get to know and trust Him. The more time you spend with God and get to know Him, anxiety and worry lose their grip. One of the many blessings of God through His Son Jesus is...FREEDOM.

Chapter Twenty-One

The Wilderness

When I finally got back to the Lord, I was so overwhelmed. I was longing to feel His love and His presence like I did when I first surrendered my life to Him at fourteen. I never thought I would feel that way again. Through the years I would have moments feeling God's presence, I just didn't have that surrendered peace. I felt like I was trying but I really was just going through the motions. I was a Christian on Sunday mornings for the hour or two I gave to the Church. I prayed regularly but I just didn't have that joy and peace that comes from abiding in Him. God was on the back burner of my life.

God will never violate someone's free will. He lets us run our lives till we come to the end of ourselves. We feel if we can just get out of debt, then we will be happy. If we could become the president of the company then we would be happy. The most common excuse is, "If I can just find a person I can share life with and fall madly in love, we can go off into the sunset and live happily ever after." We are always trying to fill that void in our hearts that only God can fill.

Read Ecclesiastes. It is Solomon sharing all he learned. He had everything—women, money, power, you name it, he had it. (Ecclesiastes 1:14): *"I have seen all the things that are done under the sun; all of them are meaningless, a chasing after the wind."* Solomon had to find out for himself that only God can fill that vacuum-sized hole in his heart.

God will not force you to have a relationship with Him. Perfect love demands nothing, it wouldn't be perfect love. If He forced us to love Him we would be like robots. I often use this scenario: I love my wife. We had been together prior to me having anything (not that I have much, but we live in a nice house and try and go on a nice vacation each year). But suppose I was rich, I would want to know she loves me for me, not for what I have or can provide. That's the same for God. He wants you to make that choice to commune with Him, to have a relationship. Perfect love has no demands. I love the picture of Jesus at the door knocking but there is no door handle. This signifies that He will not force himself in, you must invite Him in. God does pursue us:

(John 6:44): *"No one can come to Me unless the Father draws him; and I will raise him at the last day."*

(Psalm 139:7): *"Where can I go from Your Spirit or where can I flee from Your presence?"*

We are often running around like a rat in the wheel of life. We don't bother to give God a thought, because of our false perception of who He is. After coming to the end of myself, I said, "I have a beautiful wife, three amazing kids, a beautiful house, a successful career with a good company and a successful side business," and I realized like Solomon that I needed God. I was on fire but then came the "wilderness," the crushing.

While you are in the wilderness, God is teaching you who you are but more importantly who He is as well. God is showing you who you are in Him. It can be exhausting and many times you feel like giving up. I often would say, "Lord, I just want to go back to church and throw a few bucks in the offering plate, this is too difficult for me." You feel like you are being crushed with so many trials and troubles. Some of what you are going through is of your own doing from bad mistakes or bad decisions. Some are trials God is using to teach you, and some are attacks from the enemy, Satan. Things might get so bad that you give up because you know you can't fix it. That's where God wants you—to realize you can't fix it—then He steps in and fixes things His way. God always puts His signature on healing and restoring. You just sit back in awe. God doesn't promise to stop or remove every storm we go through, but He does promise to be with us through it. You learn to know and trust God in this process.

One night I was driving home from Syracuse, New York, after work. I was so defeated and upset, I said, "God, tonight, I'm not listening to any Christian music or sermons, and I'm not praying." Like a little child having a temper tantrum. The tractors I use for work have sensors so if the tractor gets close to the white line on the edge of the road a buzzer goes off and in this tractor it then turns the radio on after you get off the white line. That is to prevent drivers from falling asleep. So, I was coming back from Syracuse and all night I was sulking, feeling sorry for myself. As I was driving I ran too close to the white line and the buzzer went off and when the radio came on, Jeremy Camp's song, "I Still Believe," was playing. God was using that song to say, "I understand, Jon." Here God was showing me His sense of humor. I remember chuckling in the tractor.

God is relentless in his pursuit of us. There was another time I was going through a trial and struggling immensely. I have struggled with this book. Who am I to write a book about God? I remember thinking, *Lord, you have put so much on my heart, this book being one of them, things I just can't envision myself capable of doing.* I was going through so many external and internal struggles, under constant attack. Satan was getting into my head and saying, *"You're not enough, you'll never amount to anything."* These thoughts are not from God. Once again I was having a spiritual temper tantrum. Well, that night I ran close to the white line and after the buzzer went off, Lauren Daigle's song, "You Say," came on the radio. Once again our loving, faithful God was ministering to me. God knows everything we are going through, He knows every facet of our lives. God was showing me who He was, how much He loved me—us—and that He would get me through. Incredible that both these times the radio pops on with a Christian song.

God will push you or put something on your heart that might not make sense, and it can be very stressful because it brings you out of your comfort zone. Every year I would do a spring cleanup and mulch job for this customer who was a foreman for a major company. I would always chuckle when I heard his answering machine. The message on the machine would say, "I'm not home right now but please leave a message. But if you're a salesman or a religious nut, don't bother!" And then he would make this real funny noise. I would laugh every time I heard it. I get it, I don't like religious nuts either. Well, one year God said to me after I left a message, *"I want you to speak to him."* So, what did I do? I ignored Him. Sure enough, the next year after I left the message, God said to me again, *"Yup, I want you to speak to him."* This customer and I had a respect for each other. We were both extremely hard workers. Plus, I appreciate my customers, they are doing me a favor by hiring me. I like to go the extra mile in appreciation, and I love people. So, after I did the cleanup this year he gave me a tip.

But this year, Mr. Anderson was in a wheelchair. He had a dangerous leg infection. So, I tried to weasel out and said, "I'll keep you in prayer." I didn't share what God was calling me to do. This isn't my thing. He's a foreman, and most foremen are strong people, firm. From his message on the answering machine, I knew he didn't like religious people. He was always very nice to me but he had an intimidating personality. Foremen need to get things done so they need to be firm and no-nonsense. I chickened out. Then, one day I was reading Francis Chan's book, *Crazy Love*, and I couldn't get Mr. Anderson out of my head. I flipped the page and this is the Bible verse I opened up to:

(Jeremiah 1:7): *"But the Lord said to me, 'Do not say I am too young; you must go to everyone I send you to and say whatever I command you.'"*

It was God speaking to me and reminding me that He told me to speak to Mr. Anderson. When God speaks it is heightened, He lets you know it is Him speaking. I bowed my head and said, "Okay, Lord, I'll go." Of course I still procrastinated and within a short period of time my friend Jeff at work who is friends with Mr. Anderson and was the one who referred me to his account, came up to me and asked if I heard about Mr. Anderson. I said no. He said, "He's really sick in the hospital and it's life-threatening, they moved him to a nursing home." A panic came over me because I knew I didn't do what God put on my heart to do. What if he were to die and I didn't do what I was told to do? So, I found out where he was and visited him.

There was a woman in the room when I arrived, and somehow I just knew she was praying for him, for his salvation. Of course I could be wrong, for I have no proof, but it was a strong sense I felt. Sadly, I chickened out again and just gave him a card and gift and said I'd be praying for him, which I did. I remember after leaving, sitting in my truck thinking that the woman would do what God sent me to do. I was stressed out, I don't like doing things like this, and I wondered why hadn't God given up on me? If he can fix me, there's nothing but hope for you. I always kid with God and tell him I'm sorry I make His white hair grey. I always tell Him to just take the frying pan out of Heaven and smack me up against the head with it. One thing you will learn when you get to know God is that He is very patient.

More time passed and our family went to see the movie, *God's Not Dead*. Just before the scene at the end of the movie when the atheist gets hit by the car, Mr. Anderson comes to mind again and yes, it was God speaking to me and telling me He had a job for me to do. I prayed and told the Lord I would go. When I got home I was taking a nap on the couch and felt a strong prompting from the Holy Spirit to speak to Mr. Anderson again. I thought, *God, I'm definitely going to do what you asked, but please, I just want to rest before I go to work.* I look up and on the coffee table is Francis Chan's book, *Crazy Love*, and what was staring right at me was what's written on the book: *Overwhelmed by A Relentless God!* I just laughed. God has such a sense of humor and I was really starting to see how personal He is with us. Yes, God has a personality, and we are created in His image. (Genesis 1:27): *"So God created mankind in His own image, in the image of God He created them; male and female He created them."*

The next day I reached out to Mr. Anderson and at this point he was in a different nursing home, so I scheduled a meeting with him. I asked him if he could help me with reading blueprints from the company he worked for, which was true, but that wasn't the reason I was going to see him. Yes, the Lord convicted me not to be dishonest. When Mr. Anderson called to confirm, I shared that I wanted to talk with him about something that was on my heart, the blueprints were just a side thing if he had time. God never tolerates dishonesty, we can only speak truth. That morning before I went to see him, I was a nervous wreck. My wife prayed with me and I felt better. When I got there I shared what God had put on my heart to tell him: (1) that He loved him; and (2) that He knows every hair on his head. I shared my entire testimony, even about my sister. I don't always share about my sister because it can be more than most people can handle. He shared that his ex-wife became involved in a cult religion, and he said it ruined their marriage. He said nothing he did was ever good enough with them. They take the Bible and they twist it. There are many friendly, nice people in this organization but they are misguided.

We had a very nice conversation for a good hour and a half. He shared that he does believe but was so offended by what his wife became by this religion that it ruined their marriage. Folks, grace is a gift, we can't earn it.

(Ephesians 2:8-9): *"For by grace you have been saved through faith, and that not of yourselves; it is a gift of God, not of works, lest anyone should boast."*

(John 3:16): *"For God so loved the world that He gave His only begotten son that whosoever believes in Him has everlasting life."*

The Bible wasn't principally written for just leaders to interpret. Salvation doesn't come through close alignment with leaders. The Bible is written for everyone to read and cherish. It is God's love letter to us.

(Matthew 27:51): *"And behold, the veil of the temple was torn in two from top to bottom; the earth did quake; and the rocks were split apart."*

What this means is Jesus did it all. He took all of humanity's sin on the Cross. We no longer need to sacrifice animals on an altar and you no longer need a priest or a pastor to go into the Holy of Holies for your sins. You now have the privilege to go before God yourself through Jesus. Jesus is the only way to salvation.

(John 14:6): *"Jesus said, 'I am the way, the truth, and the life. No one comes to the Father except through Me."*

I never really found out if visiting Mr. Anderson changed anything but it was an act of obedience on my part. God was teaching me not to fear anyone. If He sends me, He will give me the words and be with me. God was teaching me to trust and obey.

When you're in the wilderness, God is refining you, shaping you. God was working on all the dark things in my heart that I didn't even know were there. I love the sermon Christine Caine preached. I think the title was called "Anointing vs. Gifting." What she said was so true. God brings you into a darkroom—the kind we used when we processed pictures. No one or any light can come in during the process of developing the film. This is what God is doing, He is showing you things in your heart you need to change, but in this process He is protecting anyone else from seeing, just you and He know your issues. He showed me where I was judgmental toward a fellow believer. He used this person I was judging in a powerful way in my life and then spoke to me clearly and in a serious tone, *"I know the heart."* He was showing me not to judge anyone, only He knows the heart. He dealt with me being critical of someone only to have this person read something so beautiful the hairs on the back of my neck stood up because I felt the words were straight from God's mouth.

He showed me a situation where I was looking for the spotlight, not giving wholly to God. This is part of the wilderness. God keeps refining us like silver and a blacksmith heating the metal till God sees himself in the precious metal. It's a painful process but when done you are usable for Him. Think about it: How can God use powerfully a person who is judgmental, critical, or self-seeking? If He uses us like that, we can cause more damage than good and hurt the name of Jesus.

That's a big problem with Christianity today. So many people who profess to be Christians are judgmental, critical, legalistic, and most importantly without love. God is love!

(1 John 4:8): *"Whoever does not love does not know God, because God is love."*

Love comes first, and the next most important attribute of the Christian should be humility. Love and humility and kindness are the three main ingredients of a genuine follower of Christ. Think about how humble God is. His Son was born in a manger, which was really an animal feeding troth. Born in a barn. He washed the feet of his Apostles. He rode into Jerusalem on a donkey. This is the Son of God, Maker of the Heavens and Earth, the stars, the galaxies. Unbelievable! We need to be the salt and light of this world, full of love and humility and kindness.

Let's venture on to a major trial which taught me how much God loves us, knows us, and is there for us.

Chapter Twenty-Two

Life Can be Extremely Hard, Thankfully, I Have God

O ur son was going through very difficult years which started in his first year of high school. He graduated junior high with an average above 90 every quarter and was a recipient of the President's Award. He was a good student without putting forth much effort. We have always been so proud of JonMichael. He is extremely loving and fun to be around. He is also very athletic, which I think was passed down from my father who received two full scholarships to college for basketball and soccer. JonMichael was gifted at anything he did but gymnastics was his most amazing gift; he was a natural.

We used to travel all over the State for competitions, and he was always at the top of his team winning many medals. He was so talented that they wanted him to start training for the Junior Olympics. I have many regrets that I didn't push him more, but it became so demanding that they wanted him there sixteen to twenty hours a week for training and it was beginning to burn him out. Plus, it was costing us $10,000 to $12,000 a year, which was a lot since at that time my wife was a stay-at-home mom and I was the only provider. I knew he enjoyed playing baseball too, and enjoyed just being a kid. Over time, he faded out of gymnastics. Satan would love to keep me feeling regretful about that, but I know God has other plans.

Among his many qualities, I admire that JonMichael's friendships are so diverse. He sees people for who they are on the inside and doesn't care about their popularity, their skin color, or their ethnic background. He is friends with everyone. I am not saying my son is perfect, but we are so proud of him, we see he is a kind, loving, compassionate young man who likes to have fun. On the flip side, JonMichael was a tough kid to raise because he always pushed the envelope and wanted his independence before he earned it. You could see his rebellious spirit, but it really began to escalate when he started high school. I think because he is such a lovable person that it helped counterbalance his becoming difficult.

JonMichael was dealing with a lot of anger issues and he would not talk to a counselor, so it was very hard to figure out what was causing his anger, anxiety, and depression. There were many holes in our walls, doors, and closets. This was very hard for me to deal with because I wasn't a perfect child either, but I was always respectful. I never damaged things, and usually if I talked back to my parents, later that day or the next day I would apologize. We were in such a tough place trying to find a good counselor and if we did find a good counselor we had to wait two months just to be seen, and then when we started the counseling, one hour a week didn't seem enough. The pressure became overwhelming and we wanted instant relief.

Remember, this is just one child, we have two others plus our own battles in life to deal with. I always say I don't know how people who don't walk with God do it. It's amazing how spending some alone time with God brings a peace that flows over you and helps you to get through the tough times.

(Philippians 4:7): *"And the peace of God, which surpasses all understanding, will guard your hearts and minds through Christ Jesus."* **This is a promise from God for those who love and fear the Lord.**

Early one morning, during his junior year of high school, JonMichael was already having a bad day, and I just wasn't in the frame of mind to deal with him slamming doors and being disrespectful. He slammed the garage door connected to the mudroom and I chased him out and told him not to slam the garage door going outside. Well, he did and somehow we got into a shoving match and as he was walking away he threatened to drive his car into a pole, so at that point I knew I had to take the keys. He wouldn't give them to me and we started wrestling on our front lawn. The whole situation was so traumatic to my wife, daughter, son, and me. Here is a son I love so much but my actions and the way things transpired pushed him away rather than pulled him in. Because things escalated so badly, I knew if I left it would help calm the situation. I had so much anguish inside, I didn't even know what to do.

I left and had no one to go to. My father, who was a great listener and was always there to pray with me, passed away a month earlier. I have so many memories of my dad wrapping his arms around me and crying, and after he pulled himself together, he would pray, "Help, Lord, Help." But my father wasn't there anymore. I love my mom and we are very close too, but under certain stressful situations she tends to try and correct or explain why something happens, and I was so broken I couldn't hear anything but grace, mercy, and compassion. I can't even explain the anguish I was feeling. So, I went to my special spot where I would spend time with the Lord. God met me there in such a powerful way and sent me on a journey. This is what I wrote to my family the following day:

Yesterday was an awful memory. I apologize for my failure to all of you. I ask your forgiveness for falling short as a husband, father, and a man of God. I started yesterday at a place where I go and seek God. We as a family have alienated ourselves from having a church home and a church family. But as I felt all alone, I prayed that God would comfort you, it was a traumatic event. But God met me there and with a soft whisper said, "Taste and see that the Lord is good," and "Be still and know that I am God." These verses just kept coming to me one after the other and I realized it was God speaking to me. I saw a vision of Time Square Church and felt led to travel down to Times Square in NYC. I have listened to over a hundred sermons while driving from Pastor Carter Conlon and at this time he was the lead pastor of Times Square Church. It was like I was on autopilot. I just got on the Thruway and drove. Many times I wondered what I was doing. I got down to Times Square Church and couldn't park my truck anywhere because it was too big. A construction worker stopped, came over, and said I could park my truck with his construction vehicles. All God!

When I got to Times Square Church, it was closed. I was reading the notice about service times and this man came out and gave me a brochure and said they were closed. He then asked if I would like to come in and talk with someone and introduced me to Evan. Evan was in his early thirties and worked there handling the building activities and working with the youth. We talked for a while and he gave me a tour and talked about the history of the church. He shared about an extremely difficult time in his life. He was sitting almost exactly where I was and he looked up and saw at the head of the church a big, massive crown in the ceiling. The whole ceiling is historic with angels all around. At one time the church was a theater used for sinful plays that people would see. The owner at the time said his plays would never be stopped. The significance of the crown is that in 1987, God would call a man from the south, David Wilkerson, to buy the theater and turn it into a church that would minister to thousands of people. Directly above the stage and the pulpit stands the crown of Jesus and in the ceiling all around are little angels. It signifies God is on the throne and God knows the future and to trust Him.

Evan then introduced me to Shawn, probably in his fifties. Shawn shared his story of how God brought him all the way up to NYC from Alabama to help with construction work in the church and he eventually came to surrender his life to Jesus. God had me meet Shawn because his relationship with his son was hindered but as he came to Jesus, God healed their relationship to something better than he could have ever imagined. God also showed me that we need friends who love the Lord. For that short period of time, I felt so much love and acceptance and part of a Christian family. It helps you get through difficult times. When we're weak, others are strong.

I then went and stayed in a hotel in Poughkeepsie. I felt everyone needed time to calm down and think. I apologize if that hurts you but I needed it for me. I put my Christian music on and went to sleep at 6:45 p.m. after an emotionally draining day. I woke up at 11:00 p.m. to

the song from Casting Crowns, "Just Be Held." That song
ministered to me.

God is on the throne and even though this is a painful
experience for us, He will fix it, it is part of His plan. I got
up this morning and felt led to go to this church I pass
every day when I leave the building in Poughkeepsie for
work each day. There I met Adam and his wife Jennifer,
an elder and administrator of the church. They shared
with me all their family has gone through and how we
have to trust God. Most importantly, they said you must
fight for your family and show them the love of Jesus.

JonMichael, I love you more than life itself, as well as
Deyvn and Jillian. JonMichael, I want to walk alongside
you and be there for you as you go through this very
difficult time in your life. My love for you is
unconditional. I am human and as your dad I'm going to
fail you at times but as the Bible says, you have a Heavenly
father that picks up where I fail, and He's perfect and
faithful and will never fail you. I believe God has a
ministry for us to do together one day where we work side
by side helping others. We both love helping people. I
believe you are in a spiritual battle and should ask God
for help. You have to hold every thought captive to Jesus.
You need to constantly renew your mind in Jesus. (2
Corinthians 10:5): "Bring every thought into the
obedience of Christ Jesus." I will support you with
unconditional love, but I believe in due time God will fix
your thoughts and what you are going through. He will set
you free!

I believe God has a specific plan for each of us in our family and for us as a whole. We need to slow life down so we can have more time together. One step at a time, as God leads. We need to change as a family, we each have our part. Love equals respect for each other. It's doing something without expecting anything in return. It's about putting the other person's needs before your own. I've failed all of you in this as we have failed each other. God needs to be on the throne of this family, and love needs to be the focus. There will need to be a lot of change and we're going to have to cut back in certain areas of our lives, but as Evan and Shawn both said, they went through so much change but they can't express the peace and joy they have walking with God. I will be in church every week, I'm also getting plugged into a Bible study and involved with church. Not sure if it will be Grace Fellowship, Our Savior's, or another church that God provides, but I'm not ever going to be alone by myself on an island alienated. That's where Satan wants us. The Bible says a house divided cannot stand (Matthew 12:25). I hope you guys will all get back to church and get involved with a good healthy youth group. We all have free will and until we give God the honor and glory He so greatly deserves, our house will be divided and have trouble standing. It's a family effort in everything from God—church, chores, cutbacks, and treating each other with love and respect. My commitment is to God, my wife, my children, and my future grandchildren.

I hope we can use this as a major turning point for our family and make our house into a home again. We have to be honest, the way we are living is not fulfilling. We have gotten away from eating dinners together and going to church as a family. This isn't the way it's supposed to be. We have somehow lost our way. We are all like rats in a wheel. We need to slow life down and spend more time as a family. When you have a chance, listen to Casting Crowns, "Just Be Held." We have an amazing God, how sad that we don't spend time getting to know Him better.

I'll see you guys a little later, I have to travel back. I love you with all my heart!

****

I am filled with gratitude for the Lord. Everything is not perfect but there have been many victories and things are going in a positive direction. I love my son and there is not one thing I would change about him. God has given him a heart to unite and kindness for others, he has a very loving spirit. JonMichael and I don't ever leave the house without a hug and saying, "I love you." JonMichael is still trying to find his way, and I have every confidence in him. I remember being where he is and not knowing what I wanted to do in life. I heard it said that depression can be linked to not envisioning a future. Sometimes as parents we add unneeded stress to our lives not realizing our kids are on their own journeys. This is when we need to love and guide them and pray without ceasing that God will protect them and draw their path to Him. Recently, he gave his mom and I a beautiful card and a gift, apologizing for all the difficulties he put us through. God is so, so good! We are so proud of him as well as our daughters, Devyn and Jillian. My wife has always said "you are only as happy as your saddest child." Thankfully, we are happy again.

I pray if you are reading this and going through a rough situation that you draw closer to God and invite Him into your life. (Luke 1:37): *"Nothing is impossible with God."* **What started out as one of the worst days of my life, a gut-wrenching, awful experience, became an amazing journey with God where He showed me how intimately He knows me and answered every question that was on my heart.**

(Romans 8:28): *"All things work together for those who love God and are called according to His purpose."* **This is another promise from God.**

My faith and love for God stirs in my heart and I am undone by who He is. During one of my darkest hours, He was so faithful. I stand in awe of you, Lord!

I want to share a special story about God's love and faithfulness to my mom in a prayer for my grandmother.

Let's detour.

Chapter Twenty-Three

Relentless Love—My Grandmother

My maternal grandmother loved to read three to four books a week, but as she read she would chain-smoke. No matter how hard my grandfather, my mom, and her siblings tried to get her to quit, she wouldn't listen. Sadly, in 1974, my grandmother was diagnosed with oat cell lung cancer, one of the deadliest forms of cancer. She was given 15-18 months to live, and remember, this was back in the 70s when we didn't have the technology and resources we do now. At this time my mom already moved to Upstate New York so she was 360 miles away. My grandmother was not a believer and no matter what my mom and her sister Jane said to her about God, she didn't want to hear it. My mom said my grandmother would make comments that God was for men and not women. She said the Apostle Paul stated that, which is false.

(1 Corinthians 7:9): *"But if they cannot control themselves, they should marry, for it is better to marry than to burn with passion."*

What I take from this verse is the calling of God on a person's life can be demanding and would require sacrifice from the spouse, and if the spouse was unwilling to sacrifice, it could hinder the work of God.

That is why we pray diligently for the right spouse so they are a blessing. Billy and Ruth Graham are a perfect example of that blessing. My grandmother had a spirit of deception which came from Satan. God hates favoritism. He does not favor men over women. (Roman 2:11): *"For God does not show favoritism."* God loves us each equally. He loves you just as much as He loved Billy Graham, Mary the Mother of Jesus, and The Apostle Paul. Yes, He gifted these men and women more for His purpose, but He loves us equally. That little seed of mistruth from Satan stopped the love of God for my grandmother for almost a lifetime.

My mom was so broken over her mother being lost and dying without knowing Jesus, she broke down in church one day. A beautiful woman in the church wrapped her arms around my mother and they prayed together. After the women prayed a beautiful prayer, my mom prayed that Jesus would become real to her mother, that He would heal her. She asked that He wouldn't take her mom until her mother was saved. My mom said she felt over time that God ingrained in her heart that He wouldn't take her mother until she was saved. *This was a promise of God to one of His children.* My mom also felt led by the spirit to ask God to send someone to share Jesus with her mother because no one in the family could reach her. They lived in a neighborhood where the houses were well separated and their house was also on a hill. I have many fond memories of that house, and we serve the God of impossible.

So, what did God do? He had a lady named Olga O'Dell move into the neighborhood. Olga O'Dell sold real estate and befriended my grandmother. Later in her disease as my grandmother started to lose her vision, Olga O'Dell would read to my grandmother and in the process show her the love of Jesus. This started the walls in her heart toward God to slowly break down. As I shared earlier, the doctors originally gave my grandmother 15-18 months to live. After about three years the doctors told my grandfather they didn't understand how she was still alive. My mom said, "Dad, I do. God promised me he wouldn't take her till she came to know Him."

My mom felt prompted by the Holy Spirit to have pastors from the area come and pray over her mother. She asked my grandfather if we could do that. He eventually agreed and my mom reached out and contacted Full Gospel Businessmen, who led my mom to none other than the same Pentecostal church that Olga O'Dell attended. They graciously accepted her invitation, came over to pray, gathered around her bedside, and laid hands on her. My mom said my grandmother felt like something was shaking her from the inside out when they prayed. My grandfather had on a flannel shirt and when they were done praying, his shirt was drenched with perspiration from the presence of the Holy Spirit. Through this experience my grandmother came to know Jesus as Lord of her life. *What an amazing God we serve!*

It took my grandmother almost five years to surrender to Jesus. Always remember, God will never violate a person's free will. God's love is perfect. Perfect love has no demands. Our job is to continually intercede for people. When we pray, we are bringing the spiritual realm down to the earthly realm. In a nutshell, we *activate Heaven*. I didn't get many years with my grandmother because she died when I was six years old, but what I remember most is she was always so loving to me. Thankfully, God sent an angel named Olga O'Dell to help in the process and one day I will see my grandmother in Heaven because of her. After greeting my grandmother, I'll give Ogla O'Dell a big hug and thank her.

One of the things I've come to learn on my journey with the Lord is so many people want nothing to do with God because of misconceptions. There are many that don't want to be bothered because the Cross demands something of them. I think it's easier to understand when you realize God is your Heavenly father and He's correcting you like a loving earthly father would do, but He is perfect without fault or error. When God corrects you, it's because He loves you and wants the absolute best for you. He's protecting you. When we see it in that context it helps to realize God is *for* you, not against you, and most importantly He loves you.

Let's take another detour and explore two attributes of our amazing God!

Chapter Twenty-Four

Faithfulness and Love of God

As I shared in the beginning of this journey, my mom would drag all five of us kids to church and we would give her such a hard time that as a little boy of five years old, I would always wonder why she bothered. Now I see the importance of the sacrifice she made. But most importantly, God sees.

My mom has been through so much, her Cross has been extremely heavy at times, she's had a hard life to say the least. But God has been so faithful! Maybe her Cross was heavy so that one of her kids would write a book about God and His love and faithfulness that would inspire many. God's ways are not our ways. We all would love the easy ride without any problems, but sometimes you learn God's love and faithfulness during the most difficult times of your life. Like C.S Lewis said, "God whispers to us in our pleasures but shouts to us in our pain." There are no guarantees of a pain-free life for anyone. No matter what my journey is, I want to walk with God.

Unfortunately, although my mother brought us to church every week, her children took a detour from God's love and tried their will instead of His. As I shared earlier, my brother died tragically but God showed me that He was with my brother, from a poignant memory of him confessing Jesus as Lord and Savior of his life. We also had a letter my brother Jimmy wrote to my grandfather saying he invited Jesus into his heart, and a third confirmation was the beautiful picture, *Welcome Home,* that the Zuelsdorfs, a beautiful Christian couple, were prompted from God to purchase *prior* to my brother's death while on vacation. God is so good!

As I also shared in an earlier chapter, my sister who was possessed has now come to walk with the Lord. Absolutely amazing! I can remember the day at church when she was baptized in complete immersion. I love Baptism with complete immersion because it signifies you go into the water with all your sin, shame, guilt, pain and past, and come out washed clean by the love of Jesus. You are a new person in Christ, plus Jesus calls us to be baptized. I jumped out of my seat and was whistling and celebrating. People probably thought I was nuts, but they didn't understand the victory that just happened before their eyes. Here was someone who told God they hated Him, then turned to Satan and invited that evil into her life. The evil God allowed me to see helped me go beyond the earthly realm and into the spiritual realm. God's faithfulness to my mom and overwhelming love for my sister broke the shackles of Satan and brought my sister into His loving arms. Doesn't get more faithful and loving than that! My sister is a genuine follower of Jesus Christ now. She's not perfect but she loves the Lord and tries to walk in a manner pleasing to Him. I am so proud of her, and I know who else smiles from above as He looks down.

My sister Laurel ran away from home at fourteen years old and was in and out of jails, rehabs, and addicted to crack-cocaine and heroin. Crack-cocaine has a three percent cure rate, which means out of a hundred people addicted to crack, three can shake it. Heroin is worse with a one percent cure rate, which means one person out of a hundred can shake it. I can't tell you how many times we thought we were going to get the call that my sister was dead. Many times, she has been in life-threatening health crises because of abusing her body. We would always say she was a cat with nine lives. Praise God, my sister is completely clean and off drugs for three years now. But most importantly, she is walking with God, with a genuine heart for Him. Yes, she has struggles, and no, she's not perfect, but she's walking with God and that's what matters.

The other day as I was in church and watched Laurel praising the Lord it dawned on me how many times my family and I gave up on her, feeling our prayers were going unanswered. I immediately repented for my lack of faith and trust and then thanked God for His faithfulness. One day my sister and I were coming back from visiting my great-nephew in the hospital and my sister Laurel shared that all the years of drugs and repeated sin put her in situations where she feared for her life. She was hanging out with the worst of the worst, these people were vicious drug dealers with no respect for human life. The father of her first child was wanted for attempted murder. But my sister said that every time she called out to Jesus, He always delivered her. (Romans 10:13): *"Whoever calls on the name of the Lord will be saved."* This is the amazing love and faithfulness of God. My sisters must always guard their hearts that Satan doesn't try to lure them back. He will always be knocking at their door, it's their job not to open it.

Just as Jesus is always knocking, so is Satan. This reminds me of a story about a backslidden girl who was trying to go backstage at a concert of this evil band and the lady checking people in wouldn't allow her to come back even though she had a pass, because she said she had a guardian angel by her side. She had a praying mother.

My dad when we were young did not know the Lord, which was why my mom had to bring us to church by herself. My parents had a lot of marital problems in the earlier years. I believe this was because the house was divided. But my mom did what the Bible said to do and represented Jesus to the best of her ability.

(1 Peter 3:1): *"Wives, in the same way, submit yourselves to your own husbands so that if any of them do not believe the Word, they may be won over without words by the behavior of their wives."*

With obedience to this Scripture and lots of prayer, God answered in his love and faithfulness once again. Our church had a guest evangelist come and speak and at the end of the service did an altar call. My father said it was like a fire was under his butt and that day he surrendered his life to Jesus. I still regularly thank God for the amazing father he gave me; I wouldn't change anything about him. I also thank God because I will see my dad again one day in Heaven. It's not a hope…it's a promise!

My middle sister has also struggled with addiction and has had three bouts with pancreatitis. The last time she had this she was cut open from head to toe to deal with the infection and had to have roughly two hundred staples to put her back together. The doctors gave her a twenty percent chance of survival. My sister shared she knows it was God that brought her through. She has since recovered and alcohol is a constant threat to her, but she has discipline to guard herself from falling prey to alcoholism again. I attended her and her daughter's Baptism at Life Church years back. I know she has a belief and heart for the Lord. Her faith isn't rock solid yet as she has shared with me, but I know God will get her there.

Thankfully, my mother's parents, her husband, and son are in Heaven, because of their faith in Jesus Christ. All four of her remaining children are working out their walks with God, all at different junctures of their journeys, but they believe wholeheartedly in Jesus. My mom would rather have a heavy cross here and spend eternity with her family in the presence of God, than to have an easy life here never to see her family and loved ones again. Most of the time to see the faithfulness of God we must look back. The longer you walk with God you will learn he is *faithful*!

Look at Job in the Bible. He lost his entire family and God gave him another family to enjoy so when he got to Heaven, he had both families with God, forever—a double blessing. No, not everyone's cross is this heavy, but however heavy the cross God calls you to bear, He will be your strength to help you carry it.

I really don't think anyone is qualified to explain the love of God. It's hard for me to fully understand God's love for *me*. I know He loves me because I've read His Word and the Bible is the complete Word of God without error. And walking with God He has shown me His love, but to fully understand the amazing, steadfast, everlasting love He has for us is too hard to comprehend. My mother had an experience where she was baptized with the Holy Spirit. She said it was like a burning fire of love consuming her and just too much to contain. She said it helped her understand God's love. Many who have had this experience best describe it as a liquid love flowing through them. Don't feel threatened by others' beautiful experiences with God, He meets us all differently. In due time He will give you a special *ah ha* moment. Remember, God has no favorites, He loves us all the same. We are all special in His eyes.

I shared earlier when my wife at eighteen years old and six months pregnant with our daughter had complications from the pregnancy and was in critical condition. When asked who to save if the time came for such a decision, my wife said, "Please protect my child." My eyes were opened to the bond of love a mother has for her child. This is a touch of our Heavenly Father's love for us.

There was that special day I had with my father when I was going through one of the most difficult periods of my life and when I stopped to see him, he greeted me at the door, wrapped his arms around me, and just cried with me. The love I felt from my father soothed my brokenness. It dulled the pain. Love conquers all.

I have felt the love of my mother and father and I am so thankful for the parents God has blessed me with. Being a parent myself, I realize how much a person can love someone. When you have children you can slightly understand the love of God for His children as we relate it to the love we have for our children. But this still doesn't scratch the surface of God's love. We all know that Jesus died on the Cross for our sins. I often think about that. I would never allow my son to be mocked, spit on, whipped, beaten, tortured, and ultimately killed for the benefit of others, even if it meant seven billion people would be saved. Think about trying to watch or allow this. Ultimately down here on earth it is hard to comprehend, but through God's Word we know He loves us.

During a very bad riot—I believe it was the Rodney King riot—a black pastor put his body over a white man to protect him from the rioters who were beating this man to death. This represents the love of God, but as moving and just as beautiful a portrait of love and sacrifice this is, it still doesn't compare to the love God has for you and me. His love is incomprehensible for our minds to grasp. Down here we just get a touch of it.

(John 15:13): *"Greater love hath no man than this, that a man lay down his life for a friend."*

God had His Son who was perfect and sinless, take our sins on the Cross and lay His life down for us. With His arms stretched out between two thieves on the Cross, one received His love and one denied it. His arms stretched out signifying His love for humanity.

His hand is stretched out to you. Will you receive it?

Chapter Twenty-Five

You are Intimately Known by God

God knows us intimately. I will share an experience. I don't want you to be discouraged if God hasn't spoken to you yet. (James 4:8): *"Draw near to God and He will draw near to you."* I like what A.W. Tozer said: "We are only as close to God as we choose to be.

I realize it has been a while since I've heard the Lord speak to me. I long to hear His voice again but I also realize I might never audibly hear it again. He speaks to us the way He chooses to, He is God. His ways are not our ways, His thoughts are not our thoughts (Isaiah 55:8-9). God is mysterious. I have felt God's presence and promptings. Lots of times God speaks to us through the Bible. The words come from the Bible and are heightened. You know it's a message directly being spoken to you through the Holy Spirit. God knows each of us intimately and speaks to us in different ways. My wife said she gets a fire in her chest. A lady I know at church gets visions. My mom says she sees the color purple. We are all so different and God communicates with us individually. He knows exactly how to reach you; in fact, He knows you better than you know yourself—He created you! You are written on the palm of His hand and your very hairs are numbered. Always remember, God has no favorites and loves us equally.

The very first time I heard the voice of God in my spirit, I was at the special spot where I go to spend time alone with God—Memory Gardens Cemetery where my brother and father are buried. When I first heard God's voice, my father was still alive so only my brother was buried there. I go to the pond at the back side of the cemetery, it's private and quiet. One day I was walking around the pond on a beautiful, sunny day, and I stopped by the big tree close to the pond. I heard the Lord say something to me but I didn't understand why He said it to me like that. I was wondering what He truly meant. This was the very first time I ever heard the Lord speak directly to me. The best way to describe it is there was a heightened silence and things stood still for a moment. It's not audible as if you would hear it with your ears, but you hear it with your heart. It's clear so there's no confusion. I was in shock. I had heard many preachers talk about hearing the voice of God, but I never thought I would. I was confused but amazed. I asked the Lord what He meant but I never received an answer that day or soon after. At this time in my life, I really had no one I could go to that I trusted to help me understand.

The church I attended at that time was Grace Fellowship and Pastor Rex was the pastor. I would trust his wisdom but he had so much on his plate that I felt uncomfortable asking for his time. This is a very big church in our area with a few other campuses. My father and I never liked to inconvenience people because as workaholics, we know the value of time. I know Pastor Rex would have accommodated me because I know he has met with many people. He's very gracious and is a good listener. Fast forward four to five years: I was watching a documentary on a man I love and admire and after hearing what he said I now understood what the Lord said to me that day. I was undone. I now understood the meaning. I was watching my youngest granddaughter Mila at the time and with her in my left arm I got on my knees and with my right arm raised toward Heaven I said, "I will go where You send me and do what You call me to do." This is how intimately God knows us. As I shared earlier, we sometimes want God to just tell us what to do but when we have faith and wait for the revelation, it's that much more special and meaningful.

Communicating with God has come mostly from my alone time with Him. (Matthew 6:6): *"But when you pray, go into your room, close the door, and pray to your Father, who is unseen."* Jesus said this! That's how important it is. Along with hearing His voice, He has given me visions and dreams, this book being one of them.

On this journey when I started reading and meditating on Scriptures daily, my Christian walk became more solid. My foundation became like a rock. I wasn't feeling like I was under constant spiritual attack. Remember, the Word of God is the only offensive weapon against Satan. The Word becomes ingrained in you and is your tool for success in the battle we call life. Try to memorize Scripture, this is a powerful tool. I remember watching a man give his testimony about having had a massive stroke and he couldn't communicate for six months. He said the only thing that got him through was all the Scriptures he memorized that fed him and encouraged him. (John 1:14): *"The Word was made flesh (Jesus) and dwelt among us."*

On this journey, small groups have been another way I have met people and have come to know God better. As everyone shares their experiences, you read and study Scriptures together. In time, with the right group you will find friends who will be stronger than a brother or sister (Proverbs 18:24), but there is a real friend that sticks closer than a brother. When you are weak they are strong. When they are weak you are strong. We help each other on this journey. The Bible says in (Ecclesiastes 4:12): *"Though one may be overpowered, two can defend themselves. A cord of three strands is not easily broken."* If we pay attention closely to God's Word, He will guide us to walk out our faith and finish this race well, as the Apostle Paul says.

I absolutely love being present at church. There is something so special about communing with others and feeling the presence of God. Yes, God's presence is everywhere and can meet us anywhere but at church weekly you are sure to meet Him. I remember a girl we went to school with shared that every time she went to Grace Fellowship she would always cry while at the service. We told her that was the Holy Spirit. I love the music in the beginning as it prepares my heart, and God starts ministering to me and dealing with or answering things I am going through. Then the message encourages and guides you. It was Pastor Rex's gift and anointing that helped me grow by leaps and bounds, along with many other preachers I listened to. Make sure you find a church that doesn't sway or compromise the Bible and preaches grace and truth. *Remember, we need to adjust our lives to the Bible, not adjust the Bible to our lives.* This can be tough and a huge sacrifice. Jesus said, *"If you love Me you will obey Me."* Make sure you get to a healthy, Bible-believing church and always attend in person if you can. You will be blessed in doing so. Online is a backup if you can't attend in person.

I want to reiterate that God has no favorites. When you start to spend time with God, He will show you how intimately He knows you. Every person He communes with differently. Yes, I have heard the voice of God, yes, I have seen a demon with my eyes, but there are many experiences that others have had too. There have been some who have experienced interaction with an angel (Hebrews 13:2)—my mom who saw a bright light and was overwhelmed by the love of Jesus. I have heard many amazing personal encounters people have had. I always love listening to 700 Club Interactive on YouTube—personal testimonies of other believers. Very inspiring. When you draw close to God with all your heart, He will draw close to you and show you how He knows you in a special way (James 4:8).

Take a moment to think about that. God the Creator of the Heavens, the Earth, the moon, sun, all the stars and galaxies—your Creator—has time for you and will show you how intimately you are known and most importantly, loved by Him.

Do you have time for God?

Chapter Twenty-Six

Encouragement From my Hero and a Few Patriarchs of the Bible

So many reading this are struggling, and if you are not, we all know someone who is. We are in a rut or we made a mess of our lives. You're feeling overwhelmed, wondering how you can fix everything. My prayer is that as I share my dad's life and many heroes of the Bible, it will set an example for you, a friend, or a person who is discouraged. My dad would always say, "If I could grab you by the shoulders, I would share all I've learned." So, let's jump into my dad's beginning and let his life grab you by the shoulders.

My dad was born in 1940 and raised by Jim and Florence Kennedy in New York City. They would later move to Baltimore, Maryland. We don't know if my father was stolen or illegally adopted, that's a story in itself. Florence Kennedy was a known con-artist and his father an alcoholic. She would appear on radio shows and say she was deserted by her family and people would feel sorry and donate money to her. My grandfather, my mother's father, before he moved to Florida, sent us an article in the local paper with another one of Florence's cries for money. The article said she raised ten kids and they all deserted her and she was destitute.

My father also had a ball which he gave to me that was signed by Babe Ruth, the famous New York Yankee and leading home-run hitter till recently, but my dad said he didn't take pride in the ball because he knows his mother probably lied to get it.

Florence, his mother, would always tell him if he wanted to know the answer to where he came from it was in the black box under her bed. Sadly, my dad never looked, and who knows if it was even there? One thing she did share that turned out to be correct was about his biological parents: one was fully Italian and the other was fully Polish, which by my dad's DNA backs that up. Because of being stolen or illegally adopted, my father didn't start school till the fifth grade. Think how hard that was. Thankfully, God sent an angel, Miss Janet Connors, his fifth-grade teacher. She was an "old-school" teacher who cared about her students. My father said she would walk down the halls with her arm wrapped around him, comforting him, as he felt so overwhelmed and scared, many times crying. She would take extra time and help him with his schoolwork. My dad said she was pivotal in his life and without her he doesn't know if he would have survived. My dad even out of school and through life kept in touch with her and would occasionally visit her. This is the power of encouragement with love!

I remember listening to a speaker who said, "Do you think that homeless guy with the sign planned when he was a kid, that he was going to be a beggar? No, he didn't. Discouragement and bad choices overwhelm people and they find themselves in holes they are too overwhelmed to get out of." When I pass these people and I feel a prompting from the Lord, I stop and give them a few dollars and let them know Jesus loves them and has a future for them. I am not concerned about what they do with the money, I just want them to know Jesus loves them and I ask their name and let them know I will be praying for them. Many are in shock that someone actually cares. Just don't ever put yourself in harm's way—most of the time these people are in public, during the day, and like I said, being prompted by the Holy Spirit. Always use prayer, wisdom, and street smarts. You don't know what an act of kindness or a word of encouragement will do for someone.

Do you know the number one attribute that people admire in a person? It is *kindness*! When you know and walk with the living God, you will become a kind person. Another thing that will happen is you will truly care about people, God's heart becomes implanted in yours, and you receive the fruits of the spirit.

(Galatians 5:22-23): *"The fruits of the spirit are love, joy, peace, patience, kindness, goodness, faithfulness, gentleness, and self-control."*

Not only will you receive the fruits of the spirit, you will come to truly care for people, and always remember, people won't ever listen to you unless they believe you care.

Some of you reading this are thinking, *I don't like the person I am.* I think everyone has a trait or two that they don't like about themselves. Don't accept it, get rid of it. Correct what you don't like. That's what I love about Jesus. When you invite Him into your heart, He comes and transforms you from the inside out. He starts the process of healing all the brokenness, pain, and what's not of Him—critical spirit, judgmentalism, pride, selfishness, jealousy, uncleanness, etc. He will guide and help you to change what your conscience is internally showing you is bringing you down. I would read the Book of James for weeks until I could control my tongue. I would write myself notes and remind myself to work on these shortcomings. Don't let anything negative come out of your mouth, it creates a negative spirit, negative emotion. I promise you, if you invite Jesus into your heart as your Lord and Savior, He will transform you. Never underestimate the power of encouragement! Sometimes you might not see with your eyes but the seed you plant will make a difference.

Back to my dad's journey.

Florence Kennedy, the woman who raised my dad, pushed him in sports hoping that would be her ticket if he made it big. My dad was extremely athletic and would receive two full scholarships for basketball and soccer to Loyola College. He was very talented at baseball as well. He would also be inducted into his high school Hall of Fame. Florence basically raised my dad thinking when he got older he would take care of her. My dad said because of his fifth-grade teacher's push and feeling so inadequate he would try and overachieve. He was extremely successful and involved in many programs at high school and college. He would receive the rank of Captain in the Army and would receive a Bronze Star for Meritorious Service.

If you were to read my dad's obituary, you would never think this person didn't start school till the fifth grade, was raised by an alcoholic father and a con-artist mother, who when the neighborhood bully was beating up her son in the Bronx would push him back out the door into the bully's hands. The involvement of an angel, his fifth-grade teacher, and staying away from self-pity and discouragement (Satan's number one tool to take you down) is what got my father through. I also feel even more influential than that was his biological mother and maybe even father were praying for him. My dad when he was young said he would occasionally go to church by himself and throw some change in the offering basket. Florence said God was the Bogeyman, so there was no one with faith leading him. But at a young age God was already pursuing him.

Feeling sorry for ourselves does us no good. If you experience hardship or a bad break, it's okay to feel sorry for yourself for a moment or two, but then grab your bootstraps, pick yourself up, and get on with it. Self-pity will only hold you down. I see so many people with talent and they get a few bad breaks in a row and then get stuck in self-pity. Negativity is of Satan. Negative thoughts create negative emotions, and negative emotions create depression. My wife and I got caught in this when we were bombarded with so many things going wrong. We were playing into Satan hands, and thankfully, we escaped. Life can be extremely hard at times. We have to make the best of it. Thankfully, with God you don't need to do it alone.

If you're feeling sorry for yourself, go out and help a blind person, help a paralyzed person, help a homeless person—you will soon find your cross isn't as heavy as others. Remember, happiness is a choice, joy comes from the Lord. The happiest people are those who are most grateful. Every day we should thank God for many things. Thank you, Lord, I can see, thank you, I can hear, I can breathe without help, I can walk, talk, hear, thank you, I can go to the bathroom without a catheter or a colostomy bag. Thank you, Lord, for your mercy, your gentleness, your patience, and most importantly your love. Thank you, I know you.

One of the many things I love about the Bible is that God used blemished people. That gives me and you hope. Noah was a drunk, Jacob was flawed a hustler, deceiver, Moses had a bad temper, Rahab was a prostitute, David committed adultery and covered it up with murder, Peter denied Christ three times, and let's not forget the Apostle Paul who persecuted and killed Christians. But wait, aren't they unqualified? No, Noah saves humanity, Jacob was faithful and became a Founding Father and the Nation of Israel was named after him, Moses leads the Israelites to the Promised Land, Rahab helped the Israelites which helped them defeat Jericho and has her place in the lineage of Jesus, David becomes the most powerful King of Israel and is in the genealogy of Jesus. Peter was called "the rock upon which His faith the Church was built," and Apostle Paul would become the most powerfully used and important man after Jesus (James 5:17).

Elijah was a human being, as we are. We sometimes think these people are fictitious characters. They are not, they are human like you and me with life's struggles and thoughts. What can we learn from this? I love what the Apostle Paul says: (Philippians 3:13-14): *"Brethren, I do not count myself to have apprehended; but one thing I do, forgetting those things which are behind and reaching forward to those things which are ahead, I press toward the goal for the prize of the upward call of God in Christ Jesus."*

For some of you, your past haunts you, or something you have said or done. You feel it's too late or you have messed up too much. If you have asked God for forgiveness with a true repentant heart, you need to accept His forgiveness. (Psalm 103:11-12): *"For as the Heavens are high above the earth, so great is His mercy toward those who fear Him; As far as the East is to the West, so far has He removed our transgressions from us."*

God says your sins are forgiven as far as the East is to the West because it is unending. Accept God's forgiveness and stop having standards higher than God's. If you have brought it before God with a repentant heart, it is finished. Matthew 27:51 says: *"At that moment the curtain, the veil of the temple, was torn in two from top to bottom. The earth shook, the rocks split."*

When Jesus died on the Cross for our sins, we no longer needed to sacrifice animals, and for some we no longer need to confess our sins to a priest or a pastor. Jesus did it all! The veil was torn in two and you and I can go straight to God with our sins, our problems, and most importantly our praise because of Jesus. What a gift! If there is one thing I have noticed it is that my relationship with God has gone deeper because I have learned to accept God's forgiveness through Jesus. I would have roadblocks earlier in the journey because if I sinned or kept stumbling with a sin I would distance myself from God because of shame I felt, and if I felt more perfect or less sinful I could earn God's love and approval. (Ephesians 2:8): It's by grace we are saved so no one can boast. If this were the case and we could earn our way into Heaven, then why would Jesus need to suffer an agonizing death on an old rugged Cross for our sin? Learn to accept God's forgiveness. God looks at our heart and yes, the closer you grow to God, the less you will sin, but we will always need our Savior Jesus Christ.

****

My father's eulogy:

I would like to celebrate the life of James T. Kennedy.

We have so many fond memories as kids—from my dad chasing us around the house with the claw hole (his hand was the claw), pinning us to the ground as we screamed in agony for mercy, or him falling asleep at the drive-ins, he would start snoring so loud that the people next to us would yell, "Would you shut that guy up!"

We have nice memories of all of us, before my brother died, eating dinner around the table sharing life together. From our family trips to the Altamont Fair or our yearly trips to Wildwood, New Jersey, for which my family and many of my siblings continue that tradition.

Our family went through some tough times when we were kids, when my dad lost his job with the State. I can remember some of the cars we would drive as a family during that period of our lives. We would put floor mats or a board over the holes in the floor, and occasionally I would pull them up and look at the road while my father or mother was driving. I can remember one car where the doors didn't work and we would have to climb through the window to get out. That's cool if you're a kid but not when you're at the Little League baseball park and your mom is climbing through the window. But through this very difficult time my father worked five jobs and showed us what a man does for his family. My siblings and I would help my dad with one of those jobs. We would get up at 3:00 a.m. in the morning to deliver papers, and I have many memories of dogs chasing me. Through all of this, our dad showed us what being a man meant. You do what you have to do to take care of your family.

Our father was always generous and caring. I remember picking up hitchhikers and giving them rides. Sadly, you can't do that these days. He taught me from a young age to give the shirt off your back if you need to. He taught me your handshake is your bond. The day my dad broke his hip he tried to tip the two ambulance drivers, but they said they couldn't accept it. But he tried relentlessly to give them a tip. I often go over to Memory Gardens Cemetery for special time to sit and pray, and as I do that I always take the high road and look down at my brother's grave. On Thursday when I was there, I looked down and saw them preparing my dad's grave. It was like my dad saying, "Go down there and tip them, son." I never had cash on me so I ran to the store and got some money out of the ATM. I rode back, walked up to the guys preparing my dad's grave site and said, "This is my dad's grave site and I know he would want to tip you and buy you lunch." They were touched, but this was who my dad was. And I know for a fact he would have tipped them.

My dad was such an encourager. Stay positive, self-pity and negativity will get you nowhere. Cross your T's and dot your I's. A quitter never wins and a winner never quits. He was a great listener also. He would say God gave you two ears and one mouth to speak less and listen more. Kelly Duffy-Clement, a family friend, shared with us at my father's wake that she was trying to think why our dad was so special to her and she said she realized he was such a good listener and he cared. My dad's best friend, Dave, shared how when he had a bad head injury and lost his game in basketball, my dad spent hours every day getting him back on the court when he felt like giving up. He shared how talented my dad was, but what I remember was my dad always saying how good a ballplayer his friend Dave was and how talented he was. He was so humble and gracious.

I think the most precious memory I have of my dad is when I was going through the most difficult time in my life. I stopped over to see my parents and my dad met me at the door, wrapped his arms around me, and just cried. It was the most meaningful moment I'd ever had with him. At that time in my life words wouldn't have helped. The Bible says, "Love conquers all." If God only gave me those moments with my dad, it would have been enough.

As we chose 1 Corinthians 13 about love, this describes my father. His greatest attribute was his unconditional love. My siblings and I will tell you how loved and special our dad made us feel. He had no favorites.

My father was so concerned for our mother, his wife of fifty-four years. He would continually pull me aside and tell me to take care of my mother when he was gone. My dad was such a good caregiver to my mom when she was sick or going through something. He always went above and beyond, putting her needs before his. He led by example. His shoes I will have trouble filling.

We as a family are so proud of my dad, not just of his accomplishments but more importantly his gentle, loving, selfless, caring, compassionate, generous, kind, encouraging spirit. We all had a great relationship with him and nothing was left unsaid. If my kids have a fraction of the love, admiration, and respect I have for my dad, I'll know my job was well done.

Our family would like to thank all of you for your thoughtfulness, kindness, love, and generosity, whether it was a kind word, a card, or having food delivered to the house. From family and friends who traveled from far away to be by our side, each act of love has helped fade the pain. Our father would have been so touched and honored for the respect you have shown him and our family. We are so grateful to all of you and with a heart of gratitude, we thank you!

My father wanted the Gospel preached at his service in the hope that those who do not know Jesus would come to know Him. It was right here at this altar that my dad many years ago surrendered his life to Jesus, and because of that, he is in Heaven with a Holy, loving God, reunited with my brother, his son, who also professed Jesus as Lord and Savior of his life. The gift of eternal life isn't a hope but a promise for those who love and fear the Lord, along with many other promises for those who love Jesus.

We all know when we leave this world we can take nothing with us, but we leave a legacy. Our dad, the head of the Kennedy family, left an incredible legacy of love. Him having the Gospel preached today is his final act of love!

****

It does not matter how bad you made a mess of your life, what kind of pit you are in, how old you are. With Christ, nothing is impossible. (Philippians 4:13): *"I can do all things through Jesus Christ who strengthens me."* There is nothing that is not forgivable with God. (Romans 5:20): *"Where sin abounds, grace abounds more."*

Jesus will transform you from the inside out, heal what needs to be healed. My father's life is an example of someone who could have given up because the cards were stacked against him, but instead rose above his circumstances and more important than all those accomplishments, he was an amazing husband and father. Our journey's most important facet is the lives we touch. Do you think I would be sitting at this computer writing this book if he gave up? Put the past, the hurts, the bad decisions behind you and become the father or mother, brother or sister, friend, person God has called you to be, you desire to be, and those that love you need you to be, and if you stumble, get back up and strive for the goal.

(Proverbs 24:16): *"For the righteous falls seven times but he gets back up again."*

Rise up, find your purpose in Him, and make a difference in your family, community, and the world. You will soon love and admire the reflection looking back at you in the mirror.

The best is yet to come!

Chapter Twenty-Seven

Become the Parent God Created You to Be

M any times, when I have listened to sermons about parenting and the important role of a father in a child's life, these sermons have brought me much guilt, regret, and pain. I listen to a lot of sermons while I drive, and there have been times I turned them off because I know I have failed in many ways and it was too painful to listen to. I know I have loved and been there for my kids but I have lost so many moments, so many memories because of my past work schedule and misconception of my job as a parent. Yes, loving my children and providing is important, but being fully involved, and *time* is just as important. Learning to communicate with my kids is essential. I have talked with other friends who struggle and have regrets, not knowing how to fix things. I sense their frustration. They had great hopes of that perfect relationship but presently things are not coming together as they envisioned. There are so many variables that can hinder us but we can only work on our part. Let's face it, parenting is the hardest job in the world and we go in blindfolded. Hang on, though, there's hope for all of us.

I want my readers to be encouraged and inspired to be the parents you want to be, no matter what your situation is. One important ingredient in parenting is if your child truly knows you love them, they will overlook your mistakes and failures. They will forgive your shortcomings. Also, remember there are no perfect parents. The first step is to correct what you're missing. Many of us have baggage from our past that hangs us up. Some have trouble expressing love, some have trouble communicating, some don't spend enough quality time, some work too much, some might have extremely difficult situations. Most likely they want to be healthy parents but don't know how and the busyness of life keeps them sidetracked. For some of us, it's going to take hard work and determination, but if you truly desire to improve, you will. The key is getting God involved.

There are many like me who until drawing closer to God didn't even know we were missing the mark. We had a misconception of what parenting should be. I always felt my job was to provide, protect, and to love, but I was missing the special important ingredient—quality time and being more involved. Growing up I really didn't know what quality time was, my family wasn't geared that way. Our family was busy and going in all different directions. However, I was okay because my parents were both very loving and affirming and my two love languages were being met.

Providing for my family was like second nature because of my work ethic. Being loving comes naturally to me for the most part, but I can have trouble expressing it at times. I can remember when my wife and I first got married we started attending her mother's church, and our oldest daughter Devyn was just an infant. At the end of the service the pastor's wife, who was part of the worship team, came to me and said she was so moved by how many times I kissed my daughter throughout the service. She said she had to stop counting. I don't have a problem expressing love to my children and now my grandchildren. I always kiss and hug them and tell them I love them and for you men, yes, even my son. Because of the way my mind is geared I struggle being caught in the moment, I struggle with work and my responsibilities consuming my life. My mind constantly wrestles with my commitments. I have come a long way and God has been patiently and gently helping me with this. I no longer feel guilty when I'm not working. I have learned to set boundaries.

I admire people who know how to balance life completely. I am constantly praying for the ability to balance life, because without that balance comes stress and regret. I have come a long way with the help of God and my wife, but I know there is still progress to be made. With a Type-A personality and my duty to provide driving me, the thought of falling short or failing is scary to me. It's a form of fear brought back from those memories I have about my parents going through a difficult financial period. Some of the baggage is good because it taught me to be responsible with money, but some of that baggage caused me to work so much to relieve that fear and try to create a security blanket. People look at alcohol and drug addictions with disgust but admire workaholism, which is just as destructive to your relationships, health, and life.

I remember going to my oldest daughter Devyn's kindergarten parent-teacher conference. I was probably twenty-four years old at the time. Mrs. Madden, an excellent teacher and a beautiful Christian, said to me, "Jon, let me spell love to you," and she slowly spelled out the word T-I-M-E. Why didn't I get it? Why, Lord? Why didn't it sink in? Why didn't I try harder to change, to correct this? I can remember a pastor sharing in a parenting sermon how his wife when their kids were very young and they were in the process of building the church for the Lord, pulled him aside and said, "You need to set boundaries and capture these special moments of your kids growing up, be an instrumental part of their lives." He got it. I'm not saying I missed every moment but I missed a lot, when work consumed my life. This is a huge problem for Type-A personalities.

I was recently at a wedding and the father of the bride is an introvert. You could tell how uncomfortable he was trying to express his love for his daughter and new son-in-law. This just doesn't come natural or easy for him, it's hard work. He has all this love for his daughter but can't express it because it's bottled up. This can be so frustrating and difficult that many just give up. Some might be struggling to be good providers, some might be doing too much, which is just as harmful in many ways. There might be roadblocks, and we know deep down we're not being the parent we desire to be; we need God to help us fix things. We are not striving to be perfect, no one is. We're striving to be the parent God designed us to be.

I remember bringing my oldest daughter Devyn to work on her first job. I only said a few words during the ride over. I had all this love for my daughter but I didn't know how to express it. After I dropped her off, I prayed, "God, you didn't give me children so I couldn't communicate with them and show them I love them. Please help me." Shortly after that prayer, my daughter and her first serious boyfriend broke up and I remember going into her room. I sat on the bed, wrapped my arm around her, and cried with her. I don't remember saying anything, sometimes words aren't needed. From that point on, things changed in our relationship.

I remember a time my son JonMichael was going through a very difficult stage and the principal called home. I was home waiting for him to get off the bus because he was going to be disciplined with strong consequences. Just before he walked into the house the Holy Spirit impressed on my heart, *"Just love him today."* I followed him up to his room, sat on the bed, and asked him what was going on. I then listened and wrapped my arms around him and let him know how much I loved him. This day God knew he needed love from me more than anything. When we get God involved and listen carefully to His promptings, the healing process starts. It doesn't necessarily happen overnight, but things start moving in a positive direction. God starts slowly chipping away at the roadblocks.

As I spent my alone time with God I would get visions of all three of my children at different times, wrapping my arms around them, kissing them, and saying "I love you." I realized this was God communicating with me.

My wife and youngest daughter Jillian went away for a vacation with family friends. I couldn't go because of work. While they were away, the Lord kept giving me this vision of my wife home from her vacation and me coming home from work late at night still in my uniform. I walk over to her side of the bed and kiss her. That night it was so late, I was exhausted, and I didn't want to wake her, so I didn't follow the prompting God gave me. A week later my wife shared that she was hurt I didn't kiss her when I got home; she felt I didn't miss her. This validated the visions God communicated to me. When we make Jesus Lord and Savior of our lives and then ask Him to help us, He will guide us. (James 4:2): *"You have not because you ask not."* He may guide you with visions, He might guide you to a book, a seminar, or by a still small voice. Most importantly, He will guide you.

Let me share two beautiful stories that will inspire you when God is involved. My son JonMichael's four-year-old nursery class had a parents' day and we were all blessed to hear this amazing story from his teacher, Mrs. Roemke. When she was done, there wasn't one dry eye in the place. Mrs. Roemke has this gentle, calming presence about her and when she finished this beautiful story we understood where it came from. Mrs. Roemke and her husband are patriarchs of Our Savior's Lutheran Church and School. Mr. Roemke was the Principal and Mrs. Roemke taught nursery school for many years. Even though they are retired, they are still very involved with the church and school and are an asset to both. They both are gifted from God with the ability to teach. I have had the privilege to have Mr. Roemke as my Confirmation teacher but recently was able to be a part of his Bible study until my work hours changed. His gifts are obvious to see. My two older children have benefited from having Mrs. Roemke as their nursery-school teacher. Our Savior's is well-known because of Mrs. Roemke and many other teachers there who have a godly presence about them. Mr. and Mrs. Roemke are both beautiful portraits of Christians. If there ever were two people gifted with a spirit of humility, it's the Roemke's. Truly very loving, godly, humble people. Let's journey on and share the beautiful story of Mrs. Roemke's father's love.

Mrs. Roemke, whose first name is Carol, said that she has learned from experience that children are very able to receive and process spiritual truths. She has seen it over and over again. One day her son Mark, who was four at the time, was playing with Legos and paused, looked up at her, and said, "Mom, I think Jesus is full of so much love inside Him that He cannot stop it from coming out." She responded, "Is that right?" Absolutely, that is right! She shared she has never heard a simpler, more accurate description of our Father's overwhelming, unconditional love. She added that children are fine theologians! The next day during her quiet time with the Lord she was reflecting on her son Mark's words and journaling. She journaled, *"When was the very first time I can remember experiencing unconditional love?"* After a few minutes she heard God call her by name, "Carol." And then He reminded her of this story:

When Mrs. Roemke was a little girl her father was remodeling their farmhouse. He was working tirelessly sanding the doors and woodwork in the kitchen. He had spent several days on this project and was so dedicated and disciplined to get it done but was far from being finished. So, when he left the room, what did Carol do? She quickly picked up his sandpaper, climbed the ladder, and began rubbing as hard as she possibly could. She wanted to finish the entire kitchen for her father before he returned. What was her mistake? She was using the sandpaper on the window. When her father returned, did he become angry? Did her father blame her for ruining the window? Did he laugh at her foolish mistakes? Oh, no. He quietly showed her that windows are already smooth, then he gently and lovingly covered her small little hand with his and moved both of their hands over the woodwork and helped her work. And what did her father do with that window? That window was never replaced. Years later she asked her father about the scratches on the window. Her father paused and smiled and shared this story with her and said he wanted the window to remain to remind him that his daughter has a deep desire to help—a heart to help.

This story about the window is a simple picture of our Heavenly Father's love. God is so patient, gentle, and loving, even when we keep getting it wrong. He just keeps loving us more. I remember wiping the tears from my eyes after Mrs. Roemke shared this story thinking, *I want to be that kind of father.* If we ever take the time to analyze, we want our parents to be patient, gentle, kind, good, and loving, and that's also what we want to be to our children. That is a picture of our Heavenly

Father. The more we spend time with Him, the more we become like Him.

I was watching the funeral of Dr. Billy Graham, and his daughter Ruth shared this beautiful memory of her father. You can watch this on YouTube. Ruth shared that after twenty-one years of marriage it ended in divorce. She moved closer to her sister but quickly got involved with a widowed man and married him against her children and parents' wishes. Within twenty-four hours she knew she had made a drastic mistake. After five weeks she fled, she was afraid of him. Ruth said she knew she needed to meet with her parents. It was a two-day drive and the whole way home she wrestled with what her parents would say or do. Remember, her father was Billy Graham. Satan would love nothing more than to tarnish or embarrass a man being used powerfully by God. Her parents live on the side of a mountain and as she wound up the mountain she came around the last bend and saw her father standing there waiting for her. As she got out of the car, her father wrapped his arms around her and said, "Welcome home." There was no shame, no blame, no condemnation, just unconditional love. She said, "You know, my father is not God but he showed me what God is like that day." When we come to God with our sin, shame, guilt, and pain, God says, "Welcome home." I remember watching this on TV filled with emotion once again thinking, *I want to be this kind of father.*

These two stories move us because they are an accurate portrait of our Heavenly Father. As I wrote about these stories I welled up with emotion. I would love to have this patience and gentleness, especially in stressful situations. This is how God designed us.

(James 2:13): *"Mercy triumph's judgment."*

(Romans 5:20): *"Where sin abounds, grace abounds more"*

(John 3:17): *"There is no condemnation in Christ Jesus."*

(Romans 2:4): *"The goodness of God leads us to repentance."*

The Bible says God is gentle, patient, and most importantly, loving. We are created in His image, we resemble characteristics of God. But it's not religion, it's *relationship*. When we spend time with God, we become more like Him. We receive the fruits of the spirit: love, joy, peace, kindness, goodness, faithfulness, gentleness, and self-control (Galatians 5:22-23). This will flow out of us and those closest to us will benefit, especially our children.

No matter how bad your situation is, God can help you fix it. It might not happen overnight but with God nothing is impossible (Luke 1:37). No matter what you need or desire in your parenting, draw close to God and let Him walk with you—whether it be to express love better verbally, emotionally, physically, whether it be to become more involved or spend more quality time. Whether it be to become a better provider or be more consistent. Maybe you need healing. God is faithful and if you put your trust in Him, He will guide you and make you the father or mother you desire to be. Just as these two men who represented God so beautifully, you too will be more like God and be so pleased with the parent He molds and shapes you into. Always remember, love conquers all! Love your children!

Chapter Twenty-Eight

Miracle for the Gentle Giant

Warren and I have been friends for a long time. We have worked with each other in our full-time job and in the past he worked with me at my side business as well. Warren was rarely ever sick besides a common cold, and even with a cold he wouldn't miss a day of work, but that changed as I started to see Warren dropping a lot of weight. I would question Warren and he would just brush it off saying he didn't have an appetite, but I also noticed he was out of breath and very tired. Then one day his lower leg blew up like a balloon and didn't look good—it was swollen and discolored and by then he was down thirty pounds. I knew something was wrong.

A friend from work got him an appointment with his family doctor who ran bloodwork on him. I was there when the doctor called and told him he needed to get over to the emergency room ASAP. I remember it like it was yesterday—October 3, 2019. I brought Warren to the emergency room. At this time, he and his wife Sue were separated. He didn't want to burden her and I knew if we didn't go right away Warren would probably find an excuse not to get to the hospital. While we were checking in, Warren passed out and I thought he was dying. The nurse was trying to wake him up and was unsuccessful and started to seek help—she was beginning to panic. I was shaking his shoulder yelling to him but nothing was happening. Finally, they got him to wake. That started a journey that he's been on ever since. Warren was soon to be diagnosed with acute myeloid leukemia, a very aggressive cancer. Here is a guy never sick a day in his life and now fighting for his life. The doctor told him without treatment he would be lucky to live six weeks.

The treatment began and after a month of giving Warren three different types of chemo, nothing was working. His bone marrow draw was showing fifteen percent leukemic cells, which is bad. Warren shared that they were going to do another bone marrow draw and send him home for a couple of weeks to rest and get his affairs in order. The doctor told Warren he had less than a twenty percent chance of survival and when he came back they were going to give him the strongest chemo and pretty much bring him to the point of death to get his body ready for a stem cell transplant. If that didn't work, there was nothing they could do for him. I stopped at the hospital knowing how serious things were and spent two hours with Warren just sharing life and my faith. Warren worked alongside me for years and I have shared my faith numerous times with him, and he knew how God was working in my life. I told him about this book since the beginning when God first put it on my heart. Little did he know a chapter would be devoted to him (nor did I)!

I remember saying two things to Warren in those hours spent with him. One was that I wouldn't trade my relationship with Jesus Christ for anything. You couldn't give me all the money in the world or make me President of the United States, nothing would I trade for my relationship with Jesus, and it's not even as close as I long for it to be, which is my fault, not God's. I then told him that when God does something He always puts His signature on it, meaning you know it was done by His hands. Before I left, I laid hands on Warren and prayed with him and over him; we also had two church prayer chains praying for him, and his dad told me he had two churches praying for him also. I remember looking back at Warren saying goodbye not knowing if my friend's days were coming to an end, but I knew the presence of God was with us during that visit. As I was driving home I got a text from Warren so I pulled over and read it.

He texted me: **If you say anything I'll beat you up (just kidding) but since we prayed I can't stop shaking uncontrollably, I moved from the bed to the chair back to the bed again thinking it would stop but I'm still shaking uncontrollably**.

I texted: **Warren, that's the Holy Spirit, that's God's signature**.

The two weeks that Warren was home he moved into his wife's apartment so she could help care for him. This crisis brought him and his wife back together with their son. I stopped over and we had pizza together and talked and before I left we prayed together. Warren, his wife, and son John invited Jesus into their hearts. Absolutely amazing! I was a part of that and it was my first time leading someone into salvation prayer. The Bible says in (Luke 15:10): *"In the same way, I tell you, there is rejoicing in the presence of the angels of God over one sinner who repents."* I was instrumental in Warren, Sue, and John being written in the Lamb's Book of Life in Heaven and one day will make Heaven their home. What an honor to be a part of that. Our friendship is now forever. Before I finished praying, I felt the Holy Spirit prompt my heart to pray that God would touch the hearts of the people at work to give generously to help Warren and Sue at this difficult time. We collected roughly $6,500, the most ever collected for someone in need at work. God is awesome!

When Warren went back after the two weeks thinking he still had less than a twenty percent chance of survival, the doctor told him he was in remission. His bone marrow draw went from fifteen percent to two percent. Anything less than five percent is remission. Praise God! Remember when Warren called me after we prayed two weeks prior, he was shaking uncontrollably? That was God's signature. Warren went back to work in January of 2020, but the cancer came back two months later. God showed up in the room that day, He brought this marriage and family back together. What was He up to? Warren started aggressive chemo and for the next year battled with chemo and radiation. In May of 2021, he went to Boston and had a stem cell transplant with his younger sister being the donor. Four months later, the day before I came down to The Billy Graham Training Center at The Cove to do more writing, his wife let me know his bone marrow draw came back and Warren was cancer free. Praise You, Lord!

We don't always understand God's ways. (Isaiah 55:8-9): *"For my thoughts are not your thoughts, neither are your ways."* With Warren, Sue, and John inviting Jesus into their hearts as Lord and Savior, no matter what happened, it was a win-win situation. Why? Because they will now spend eternity in Heaven together when their lives here on earth end.

I ask you, do you know Jesus and is He your Lord and Savior? Do you love your family in life? Society says everyone goes to Heaven, and that's exactly what Satan wants you to believe. (John 14:6): *"I am the way, the truth, and the life. No one comes to the Father except through Me."*

Folks, life is so short. The Bible says, (James 4:14): *"You do not know what will happen tomorrow. For what is your life? It is even a vapor that appears for a time and then vanishes away."* Salvation is the ultimate gift, but getting to know God here is a priceless gift. No, it's not the absence of life's trials and issues, but God walks with you through them. I've learned a lot being a part of the Ogdens' journey. God is good and I have now gained two more friends in the process. Please continue to pray that this awful cancer never comes back and God will heal and bless Warren's beautiful family. Thank you, Lord, for allowing me to see the work of your hands!

Let's travel on.

*Quick update, October 2022. Praise God, Warren is still cancer free one year and five months after his stem cell transplant. God is good! Please keep Warren and his family in your prayers. We are to pray without ceasing (1 Thessalonians 5:16-18).

Chapter Twenty-Nine

Finding your Giftedness

G od has designed us all differently. Every person is special and is gifted by God. So many times in life we see people whose gifts stand out, such as a professional baseball player, football player, or a singer. I think most of us admire these gifted people and in many circumstances we wish we had their gifts. I know we all would love the gift of being able to sing. There's nothing better than a beautiful voice. Music has the gift of motivating us, reminiscing about our past, it can make us happy or sad. Many times God has spoken to me through music. But so many times we take for granted the gifts God has given us.

From a little boy I struggled in school. I was excellent at math till I hit high school, but reading comprehension was always a challenge. I now know it's because I had Attention Deficit Disorder. I don't think they even diagnosed it when I was a child, but I think I had it. I never understood anything I was reading because my mind was on the playground or somewhere else, but because of this I always felt inferior. I always felt that lots of studying or college was too much of an uphill battle. As I have gotten older my mind has slowed down and it has gotten better, but I still find myself reading things two to three times because once again I start thinking about something else.

When I was thirty years old, I went to school for a semester because like one of my closest friends, Eric, I wanted to be a police officer. In one semester while working full-time I was able to get ten college credits and I got another eighteen by clepping. Clepping is studying for the exam and if you pass it you get the three college credits. So, in one semester's time I got twenty-eight college credits but I decided to just stick with the company I was with. I already had eleven years with them and their health benefits, pay, and pension were excellent. As I look back I believe I made the right decision because I startle easily and I might have been trigger-happy. That would not be good as a police officer. I still occasionally dream I'm a police officer; there's something about those lights I've always liked. But I always enjoy the dream. Love and pray for our police officers. They have the hardest job in our world today, along with our military.

I remember reading a book or hearing a sermon about a guy who was visiting his neighbor and his neighbor was working on his mower. The guy said to his neighbor working on his mower, "I could never do that." The neighbor working on his mower stopped what he was doing, looked up at him, and said, "That's because you haven't tried." We really can do almost anything if we put our mind to it, and with Jesus all things are possible.

I learned at an early age that if you want something, you need to go for it yourself because it will not be given to you. Our family went through a very difficult season which helped direct me. This was part of my childhood when my father lost his job. When my mom brought me to baseball, I would have her drop me off then go park the car because the doors never worked. It was okay for me to climb out like the *Dukes of Hazzard*, but not my mom! I remember one mortifying moment when the door fell off the green Pinto in the parking lot. *Help!*

Make it go away! All kidding aside, now I wouldn't change those experiences for the world as they humbled me and shaped me into the person I am today.

My wife and I live well, but we never forget where we once were and because of that we have compassion for those that struggle. We have raised our children to be caring and kind, which is caught and not taught. My son JonMichael while working at Dunkin Donuts helped this blind, homeless man who was drunk and getting sick in the bathroom by giving him a towel and a drink and offering him something to eat. I was so proud of him when I heard this story. Little did I know that a year later I would have a special experience with that same man and it didn't dawn on me till later that day that it was the same man my son helped.

I was pulling out of the grocery store parking lot and I saw this blind homeless man. I pulled over and felt led to give him some money. I let him know how much it was so no one would take advantage of him and see if he needed anything. I also shared that Jesus loved him. He asked for a ride and on the way to the store he started to break down crying, saying he was so sorry for drinking too much and for his drunkenness. I didn't say anything to him about his drinking, but he saw the love of God through me and God's goodness. (Romans 2:4): *"The goodness of God draws us into repentance."* When we got to the store I got out of the car and laid hands on him and prayed over him and let him know Jesus loves him and his love is unconditional, not based on performance, that he needed to ask God to help him with his alcoholism and **not to run from God but run *to* Him**. I haven't seen that man since but I know he knows Jesus loves him and I still pray for him. I am moved that my son and I were called to represent Jesus to the same man at different times.

As I shared in my dad's eulogy, my dad taught me that a man does what he must do for his family. My dad worked five jobs for a long time and we always had a roof over our head, clothes on our backs, and food on the table. I can remember being about six years old going door to door asking people if they had any work for me to do for money. I soon learned how to work hard; it came naturally. Physical labor was second nature to me. At eight years old I would push my mower down the street a half mile to mow a big lawn for $8 and push it three quarters of a mile to mow a lawn for $6 dollars. I eventually had the concept that if I mowed 40 to 100 lawns a week I would make a lot of money. In high school I bought a business from a guy in our neighborhood and that's when I started landscaping. I've been landscaping for over thirty years and till just recently I'd taken it for granted. I'd never realized that being able to landscape and run a business successfully is a gift. Being able to transform a customer's yard into a backyard getaway is a gift.

I installed a raised patio that stepped down to a lower patio with a firepit and a sitting wall, and landscaped around it. My friend Dan came over and saw it, really liked it, and told me this was his sister-in-law Amanda's old house whom we are also friends with. When she saw it she said, "We would have stayed here if we knew we could have transformed the backyard this way." I was flattered but I still didn't realize it was a gift to do this kind of work. I love and enjoy landscaping. I enjoyed taking the patio and retaining-wall certification classes because hardscape work can be a passion. I love when I finish and admire the way the job looks. I can look at landscaping books for hours just enjoying the beauty of it. Because of a change in dynamics, I have had to put the side business on the back burner possibly till I retire from my full-time job, but I will share an experience that opened my eyes.

One day I was landscaping the front of a customer's house and she was so happy and elated with the way things turned out, she told me how talented I was. It's crazy. I had heard it many times before but now I understood this was a gift. It was an *ah ha* moment. God used the kind words from this customer, and she also did one of the most thoughtful, generous things that I will always remember. I always looked at her two sons as an example. They are both engineers and extremely bright men (my age), well-raised, good people. They both hire me for landscaping projects at their houses and have been very good to me over the years. I looked at them as gifted because I knew how smart and successful they were. Yes, they were brilliant and gifted but at their mother's house it finally sunk in that what I had was also a gift. We are all geared differently. My friend Danny can do anything. *Anything* his hands touch turns to gold, but Dan has asked *me* to help with his landscaping at times. I could never be a doctor, lawyer, or an engineer, because that was not God's plan for me.

It's funny when I meet people who don't have a green bone in their body and have no idea what to do with their property. To me it's like second nature to transform it into something nice. There are occasionally some jobs where I have to go into deep thought for ideas and even pray for God's help, but it eventually comes together. Little do my customers know that they hired a man who loves the Lord, so they also have an evangelist on their front lawn. We're not all called to be in full-time ministry, our life is our ministry. I can't tell you how many times I have shared my faith with my customers or prayed with them, or pray for them and they don't even know. If you're struggling in life or you know someone who is, you need to find your purpose.

When you get involved with a church, you will learn to see the spiritual gifts God has given you and they will be easier to use. Your life giftedness can take some intense thought if it isn't obvious, but it's there. A man that was a part of our family's life for a season said that every year he gets away by himself for a day and shuts off everything and everyone. He quiets life and examines his soul. I totally agree. Sometimes the noise of life and the busyness can choke out God's voice and our own internal voice. I suggest this for everyone. Get away by yourself for a day or two and examine your life with God. As you draw close to God, the puzzle of your life will come together. Ask God to help you find your gift and purpose. Your gift could be a homemaker, a secretary, a teacher, a banker, etc. Your giftedness and calling doesn't have to result in wealth but will be satisfying and give significance. Success—your calling—is liking what you do and being good at it. You have potential which God has gifted you with, make sure you apply it. Potential is lost when effort isn't applied. We all open our giftedness in our own time, and as you journey with God, you will be pleasantly surprised where it leads.

Let's journey on and encourage you.

Chapter Thirty

The Sweet Spot of
the Christian Walk

When you feel you are wandering in the wilderness, God is dealing with you and getting the "junk" out of your life. He is also teaching you to trust Him, to get to know Him. This is preparation for your calling; remember, not everyone is called to full-time ministry as their livelihood. You can be used just as powerfully by being a true Christian. The Apostle Paul came of his own accord and took nothing from the people he ministered to—he was there because of the love of Jesus. This Scripture jumped off the pages of the Bible as God spoke to me. I felt that God was calling me to do something I wouldn't take money from but would be providing for myself. This was a piece of the puzzle. Obviously, God can change this but I've always felt that ingrained in my spirit.

I won't take a dime from this book if it ever does sell. I want everyone to know I have no ulterior motives. Any profit will be given back to glorify God. Please don't misunderstand me, I think people in ministry should be paid appropriately, that's why it's so important that people tithe to the church. Ministry is not a job, it is a calling. Make sure you are praying for your ministry leaders, encouraging them, and if God puts it on your heart to bless them, follow through.

Years ago, I was reading the Book of Malachi and the Holy Spirit penetrated my heart on two things: (1) my tithe; and (2) my time spent with Him. In the Book of Malachi, God is very upset with people. They were bringing sick, crippled sheep to his altar. This is God, the Creator of the Heavens, the Earth, the universe! God was like, *"How dare you, I am the Holy, Holy, Holy, all powerful, loving God, and you are going to throw sick, crippled sheep on my altar."* Think about how that dishonored God. This woke me up! We are supposed to give God the first fruits of what He has provided us. I started tithing on my net income and I have prayed that one day I'll be able to give a lot more. *I promise you, when you get to Heaven you won't feel you gave too much. You will wish you gave more.*

I remember being a little behind on my tithe and I was going to do a partial payment one week and get caught up the next week. I felt a strong impression on my heart to get *completely* caught up this week, which I did. That week in church we had a guest pastor and after the collection he was walking up to the altar and stopped, lifted the baskets of money toward Heaven, and thanked and dedicated it to God. I felt so warm and that God was proud of me. God sees and hears everything we do. It's all about our heart. I make you a promise too, you'll never out-give God.

(Malachi 3:10): *"Bring the whole tithe into the storehouse, that there may be food in my house. Test Me in this,"* says the Lord Almighty, *"and see if I will throw open the floodgates of Heaven and pour out so much blessing that you will not have room enough for it."*

God doesn't need your money, it's about trust and faith. God can touch one or all of the richest people in the world and have them surrender. He owns everything. Having a lot of money is not evil; the *love* of money is evil. Yes, we are to enjoy it, just don't make it an idol and use it as a blessing. There's no greater feeling than blessing people who are struggling. There are so many rich people that distance themselves from God because they read the verse in (Matthew 19:24): *"And again I say unto you, it is easier for a camel to go through the eye of a needle, than a rich man to enter into the Kingdom of God."* (Mark 8:36): *"What good is it for someone to gain the world, yet forfeit their soul?"*

News flash! Compared to a third world country we are all rich. I feel that Jesus is saying you can't buy salvation and you can't love money more than Him. When you start to tithe it creates a bond between you and the Lord and prevents money from having a hold on you. Since I started tithing I no longer stress about money like I used to, which I shared was caused by the baggage I carried from childhood. Tithing freed me. Humanly that makes no sense, but God says, *"I honor those who honor Me"* (1 Samuel 2:30). Trust and obey, for there's no other way to have love in Jesus. **Rich people run *to* God, not *from* him**. You will be so glad you did!

The other conviction from the Holy Spirit was my time. God was getting the crumbs of my life. I now start every day with God, He comes first. If occasionally something arises, I make sure I make up that time. I am still a work in progress as God is still helping me balance life. One of the many things I love about God is He is so gentle with us. Not to mention reading God's Word every day is like food for your soul.

(Job 23:12): *"I have treasured the words of His mouth more than daily bread"*

(Jeremiah 15:16): *"When Your words came, I ate them; they were my joy and my heart's delight, for I bear Your name, Lord God Almighty."*

Again, when you read God's Word daily, it creates a solid foundation. Remember, most of the time God speaks to us through His Word. You will know when He is doing this as the words seem to jump off the page and they speak to your spirit. Most importantly, the Word is the Sword of the Spirit which is what you need to battle Satan. Remember, every time Jesus was tempted he quoted the Word of God. Ever since I started reading God's Word daily, I have walked in harmony. I'm not walking defeated but victorious in Christ. *Please read the Word of God every day, I promise you won't regret it!* Reading and studying his Word daily, spending alone time with God with no disturbances, and attending church regularly will get you to the sweet spot. Joining a small group will help you grow immensely and you might find a good friend to share life with. It's not the amount you read or the amount of time, it's the quality of it. The final action to get you there is *surrender*.

Surrender is the scariest part of the Christian journey. This is surrendering your will for God's. This is saying, "Lord, my life is Yours and do with it as You please." God will never force you to surrender your will, He waits patiently. When you finally yield to Him, the battle is over and you're now walking in complete peace and joy with God. You feel the favor of God, you feel invincible, safe, and most importantly close to God. I know this scares some of you, and believe me, I agree. One thing I can say is God is so loving and gentle in this process and the best thing to do is be honest with Him. God is teaching you *trust*. The more you get to know God, the more you learn to trust Him. God's will is your calling and that's what you were created for, that's where the joy of this life and your journey is. However, as it is written, (1 Corinthians 2:9): *"What no eye has seen, what no ear has heard, and what no human mind has conceived the things God has prepared for those who love Him."*

Everything God does is perfect. Like the beauty of a rose, a beautiful blue sky, or the sun glistening on the lake—God's will for your life is perfect.

Let go, give it to God.

Chapter Thirty-One

Buckle up, Hell or Heaven

This will be a very tough part of the journey, but is extremely important because it's a warning you need to heed. Please promise me you'll stay on till the very end of the ride, it will be worth it, with the right decision. So, let's buckle up, hold on, you're one decision away from where you will spend eternity.

As I shared in Chapter Six, what God allowed me to see in my sister was absolutely horrifying. Words can't describe the scary, pure evil we are up against. God allowed me to see into the spiritual realm. My purpose for writing this book is in the hope it will encourage you to strive for eternity with Jesus in Heaven rather than spending eternity in Hell with Satan. There may be some reading this book who might not be here in a year, months, or possibly tomorrow. Life is fragile and has no guarantees. I will be accountable before God one day for everything I brought forth in this book. Some of you reading this know me personally and know I am very honest, my family especially. I am not perfect, yes, I sin and fall short of the glory of God; yes, I have a past, but I strive to live a life pleasing to God.

I think we have all woken up to how fragile life is with the COVID crisis. I woke up to the fragility of life when I was a twelve-year-old boy and my brother died tragically. You realize there are no guarantees in life. My daughter Devyn's friend's mother had a nice conversation with us when she picked up her daughter one day, and she was dead the next day. She had an aneurysm pumping gas and dropped dead. I've listened to a well-known pastor preach a sermon and he said he was at the grave site talking with two gentlemen and both were dead within two days of that funeral. Through my career I have taken jobs driving the highways and one night this tractor-trailer passed me and up ahead right in front of me crushed a car, stopped dead in the middle of the highway. If he didn't hit it, I probably would have; there was no way of seeing it with her lights off parked in the middle of a four-lane highway in the dead of night. I literally watched the person in that car get killed right in front of me. Sadly, from a news article I found out she did this on purpose and committed suicide. I've seen numerous body bags driving the highways over the years, some very graphic. The last one I saw had a pool of blood that ran a good ten feet as a young man got crushed from a tractor-trailer. This stuff takes a little while to get over, very disturbing. I always pray and hope the person is in Heaven but I always wonder, *Did this person just die an agonizing death and now is in Hell?*

Life is dangerous. Between sickness and tragedies, we are lucky to live till our late seventies or eighties. I know this is making some of you very uncomfortable but I cannot disregard the truth of the Bible as if it doesn't exist. Society wants to tell everyone, "Oh, he or she is in a better place." That's exactly what Satan wants you to think—that everyone goes to Heaven. It's scary that some people don't believe Hell exists. That's another lie Satan wants you to believe. For every verse in the Bible on Heaven, there are three verses on Hell. Jesus talked about Hell more than any other person in the Bible did. He describes it in great detail. Read the Gospels, he says it's a place of eternal torment, gnashing of teeth, unquenchable fire, and from which there is no return (the gospelcoalition.org). I hear people nonchalantly say they will "party it up" in Hell with their friends. I promise you that won't be happening and it's no joking matter. Hell is real.

I've heard many preachers' stories of being present while an unbeliever passes and it's not a pleasant ending. I remember hearing about a nurse's experience at the bedside of a dying man that as he was passing rose up in the bed terrified then hunched over. I know this is scary stuff, but it's true. Hell is real. Remember when I saw that demon in my sister? The only thing I took away from that day was, *if there's a Devil, then there's a God.* Come on, folks, seriously think about it, why would I take my time, money, and resources to share this with you if it wasn't true? I have better things to do with my time. I'm an extremely busy person. Those that know me, know that. I have nothing to humanly gain from this book. More importantly, God's Word speaks of both Heaven and Hell. As I have drawn close to God in these last twelve years, He has placed this burden on my heart to write, especially this chapter. Understand it as if a bridge has collapsed and I am in front of it waving people to stop, trying to protect them from their doom. What kind of person would I be if I didn't give you some kind of warning?

I have great remorse when I think of the few people who recently died with whom I've interacted but never shared Jesus. Sadly, so many people are so standoffish that it's not possible, and many have hurt the name of Christ because they have been hypocrites and judgmental. Hopefully, this book has helped you see what a genuine Christ follower should be—loving, humble, kind, compassionate, gentle; no, they aren't perfect, but they are genuine and the love of Jesus should exuberate from them. Please remember, Christians can have bad days too. They are human and can fall short of representing Jesus as well.

Remember, you are not following Christians but following Jesus. Look at the pure evil of Isis, the Taliban. These people are as close to what Satan looks like—beheading people and raping women, torturing men and women—these people are sick and *pure evil!* Hell is even more evil than this.

My oldest daughter worked with this girl Sarah when she was waitressing and she told my daughter she was in a bad car wreck and died for a few moments and saw black evil spirits all around her. She said it was horrifying, but she didn't know what to do about it. Where are we Christians? We all have to wake up. There are so many people who are lost and don't know there is a God that loves them. I get it, I don't believe in beating people over the head with the Bible either, it doesn't work that way. *You will never argue someone into being a Christian.* You can't force-feed people, but the way we live can open their eyes to create a curiosity for what shines from us, and then the door opens to introduce Jesus.

We as Christians are never to play the role of the Holy Spirit and try to bring conviction on a person, we are never to play the role of God and judge people, we are to represent Jesus and love people without condemning them. Taking on the role of the Holy Spirit or God only pushes people away from the God who loves them. We also need to be obedient as Christians if God prompts us to speak up or act no matter how uncomfortable it may be. I shared in a prior chapter how God had me speak to a foreman of a major company. It was very uncomfortable but when done I knew I was obedient to what God called me to do. There is no greater feeling than God being pleased with you.

Think about this verse in the Gospel of Mark. (Mark 5:10): *"The demons that are possessing this man ask Jesus not to be sent back to Hell."* That's how bad Hell is, even the demons don't want to be there!

I hear many people say, "How can a loving God send people to Hell?" First, you have to step over Jesus to get there. Let me know if you think this is fair. God is love and God is light. So, would it be fair if you were sent to a Hell absent of love, which is God, and absent of light, which is God? Would that be fair? Think about the people who want nothing to do with Him here—why should they spend eternity forever with Him? Luke 12:47,48 hints at degrees of Hell. I do believe there are degrees of Hell and I believe I have heard a well-known preacher say there is too, but just plan on the endless burning, endless thirst, gnashing of teeth, and complete separation from God. Just separation from God horrifies me. The thought of God not hearing my voice is all I would need, but the thought of being around demons for any fraction of time and absence of God's presence, especially forever, is too terrifying to comprehend.

We are one decision away from spending eternity in Hell. Like I said earlier, you must step over Jesus to get there. Everything in the Bible from beginning to end is God's redemptive love for us. God is constantly pursuing us, but so many of us choke out His voice. Did you know every time you think about God, that's Him pursuing you? You reading this book has not happened by chance, it's in your hands for a purpose. God's trying to get your attention. (John 6:44): *"No one can come to Me unless the Father who sent Me draws him. And I will raise him up on the last day."*

I love what Charles Spurgeon, a powerful preacher in the mid-1800s said, "When the Creator gives His creature the power of thirst, it is because water exist to meet that thirst. When He creates hunger, there is food to correspond to the appetite. Even so, when He inclines men to pray, it is because prayer has a corresponding blessing connected with it." (http://www.goodreads.com/quotes/9973099-when-we-the-creator-gives-his creature-the-power-of-thirst)

God has put that instinct in your heart to call out to Him in your time of trouble because He is there in your time of need. Folks, even to your last breath God will pursue you. Only your pride and stubbornness can get in the way. I shared in Chapter Eighteen about that special experience God allowed me to be a part of with a lady dying of cancer. She probably all her life denied or blocked out Jesus, but God in His love and mercy had a special neighbor hire a landscaper and give her one more chance to receive Him, and thankfully, she did.

Many people have trouble comprehending that God is Holy. God is so Holy he cannot tolerate sin (Habakkuk 1:13): *"But you are pure and cannot stand the sight of evil."* God is so Holy He can't even look at sin. He is so Holy we can't even look at Him or it would kill us while we live here on earth. In the Old Covenant a priest would go into the Holy of Holies once a year to offer the blood of sacrifice and incense for our sins. Legend says they would tie a rope around the priest's ankle so that just in case he died in the presence of God, they could drag him out. In the New Covenant, thankfully, Jesus did it all! Jesus, the Son of God, perfect and without sin, was mocked, spit on, whipped, and died an agonizing death on the Cross for our sins. His death was ugly because our sin is ugly. God hates sin, but loves the sinner. Jesus rose on the third day and conquered sin and death…It Is Finished. That's why He made a way for you and me. We are saved and made holy by faith in Jesus (John 3:16).

John 3:16, in my opinion, is the most important verse in the Bible. I shared earlier about the time I asked God in a panic after reading a

196

Bible verse if my brother was with Him. God gave me a very poignant memory of my brother confessing Jesus Christ as his Lord and Savior. Some of us remember the Tim Tebow story of the Holy Spirit leading him to write John 3:16 under his eyes in the 2009 National Championship football game. After winning the game he found out 94 million people Googled "John 3:16." Three years later he is playing for the Denver Broncos in a playoff game against Pittsburgh Steelers which they won, but most intriguing is that he threw for 316 yards, yards per completion were 31.6, his yards per rush 3.16, the ratings for the night were 31.6, and the time of the possession was 31.06.

People, God is trying to get our attention! God is trying to get the attention of this country and the world. HELLO, THERE IS A GOD WHO LOVES YOU! (www.1cbn.com)

As I shared in Chapter Nineteen, when I was in the elevator with Jason, the Holy Spirit clearly said to me, *"Pray that Jason and Anna come to know Jesus Christ as their Lord and Savior."* That is John 3:16. And don't forget John 3:17: *"For He sent His Son into the world not to condemn it but to save it."*

I hear so many say they are good people. (Isaiah 64:6): *"But we are all as an unclean thing, and all our righteousness are as filthy rags; and we all do fade as a leaf; and our iniquities, like the wind, have taken us away."*

The angels stand around the throne of God saying, "Holy, Holy, Holy are You, O'Lord." Isaiah, a prophet of God, is someone who has spoken for God; he was undone in the Lord's presence and Isaiah said, "I am a man of unclean lips." When Peter, James, and John went up the Mountain of Transfiguration with Jesus, His face shone like the sun and his clothes became white, and when the Lord spoke in a bright cloud, the disciples fell facedown; they were terrified. God is Holy and without sin. Thankfully, He gave us Jesus and because of Jesus we will one day be able to stand in the Lord's presence.

The Bible says if your hand causes you to sin, cut it off. If your eye causes you to sin, pluck it out. The point of this is sin separates you from God. We are not going to be perfect but if you're caught in repeated sin and not trying to surrender or deal with it, you are making a mockery of what Jesus did on the Cross. It's like the old Mafia movies when the head boss just gets done having people killed, then he's at Confession like it's no big deal and later that night he has a meeting with the family to discuss killing more people. That's an abuse of grace. Grace is not cheap, it cost God greatly, His Son Jesus an agonizing death that caused him to sweat blood. If you keep living in repeated sin with no regard to God's Word, you choke out the voice of God and harden your heart. I know we all have struggles. Ask God for help.

I was having trouble surrendering sin in my life at one time and I gave it to God and asked Him to help me. Be honest with God, even if you really don't want to give it up. I needed Him to help my heart align with His and to make me strong enough to fight it. The best thing to do is say, "Help, Lord, Help." Remember, we must try to be like Jesus, crucify our fleshly desires that are contrary to what God's will is for us. We can't have the Crown before the Cross. Always remember, sin has consequences, and sadly some can be lifelong. I like the saying, "Sin will take you further than you want to go, keep you longer than you want to stay, and cost you more than you want to pay."

Jesus says, (John 14:15): *"If you love Me, you will obey Me."*

Some of you are feeling pressure and panic as you read this—don't! **Don't run from God, run *to* Him**. God will help you lay it down. God is gentle and patient and long-suffering, most importantly, He loves you! Yes, you have your part to play, but He will be at your side and love you through the process. To encourage you, I can think of at least two sins that had a grip on me and I never thought I'd get free from, but as I write this I am free and clear of those shackles. (Luke 1:37): *"For with God nothing is impossible."*

Society has done such a good job at making fun of "born again" people, trying to create an image that they are creepy. *Read this carefully*: You cannot enter Heaven without being born again. (John 3:3): *"Very truly I tell you, no one can see the Kingdom of God unless they are born again."* You are born again when you invite Jesus into your heart as Lord and Savior. When you invite Jesus into your heart, a new life begins. He starts to transform you from the inside out and transform you into His image. Your old life, sin-wise, passes away. It's a new beginning. One of the many beautiful things of now having Jesus Lord of your life is you don't have to fear Hell. You inherit salvation in Christ and will spend eternity in Heaven (Ephesians 2:9). Salvation is not a reward for the good things we have done, so none of you can boast about it. It is free, you as a believer have been written in the Lamb's Book of Life. You are a citizen of Heaven now, no fear of Hell or dying. You are free, you are exempt from condemnation and judgment.

(Romans 8:1): *"Therefore, there is no condemnation for those in Christ Jesus."*

(John 3:18): *"There is no judgment against anyone who believes in Him. But anyone who does not believe in Him has already been judged for not believing in God's one and only Son."*

I heard Pastor Steve from Bethel Full Gospel Church preach on this and it never dawned on me before. In Genesis, the first Book of the Bible, God had Noah build one door through which all animals and humans had to pass. This is also signifying Jesus is the only way.

God is pursuing you but you might harden your heart so much that you can't hear His voice. That is *horrifying*! (Genesis 7:16): "The Lord shut him in". That door only closes for you once your heart here on earth stops and if you haven't accepted Jesus Christ as your Lord and Savior, you are eternally separated. Some say, "I'll accept Jesus on my deathbed," but my brother didn't have a deathbed, he died tragically. *Settle it now.*

In recent years I have known of three people in my circle who have died suddenly. Research "died suddenly," your phone will blow up. So much so that I believe they just made a documentary called, *Died Suddenly.* We never know when our time is up. I remember a preacher sharing a story about a young man in his early twenties. He asked him if he wanted to invite Jesus into his heart but the boy said he wasn't ready yet, he wanted one more weekend to "live it up," and they would get together early the following week to make this decision. That weekend the boy died tragically. *Today* is the day of salvation. If you haven't made that decision, resolve that now. (Psalm 95:8): *"If today you hear His voice, harden not your hearts."*

Let's take a quick glimpse of Heaven before this ride is over. Heaven is not some mythical place, nor is it a fairy tale or a fantasy. Heaven is a real place where the Lord God Almighty dwells, where you are overwhelmed by His presence and love. As we see God's creative beauty here on earth, whether it be the sun glistening on a lake, the power and beauty of the waves crashing on the beach, the beautiful ocean in the Caribbean, the majesty of the mountains, the beauty of a rose, nothing will compare to the splendor of Heaven. Heaven will have pearl gates and streets of gold. Precious stones like a jasper stone, clear as crystal, and pearl gates will be a part of the beauty of Heaven (Revelation 21:10-11&21). There will be no more tears, no more sorrow, no more pain. No more death. You will be in the presence of God, face to face with Jesus, overcome and engulfed by His love.

(Revelation 21:9-11): *"Heaven will be filled with peace, joy, and praise. There will be no sadness, no pain, no death, and no fear."*

(Revelation 21): *"The glory of God and the light of the Lamb will be its illumination."* Heaven will be too beautiful for words.

(1 Corinthians 2:9): *"What no eye has seen, what no ear has heard, and what no human mind has conceived, the things that God has prepared for those that love Him."*

You will be reunited with your loved ones who made Jesus Lord of their lives. And for all you pet lovers, I believe the animals you cherished and loved will be there too. There are many references throughout the Bible about animals in Heaven. An older gentleman at church shared a story about his wife who had clinically died; she saw a loved one and her dog greeting her in Heaven.

(Matthew 7:11): *"If you, then, though you are evil, know how to give good gifts to our children, how much more will your Father in Heaven give good gifts to those who ask Him!"*

God is an awesome, loving God, and Heaven will be incredible! I hope and pray that rather than step over Jesus and spend eternity in Hell, you grab Jesus' hand and step into Heaven.

The choice is yours.

Chapter Thirty-Two

The Mercy of God

I sent this book to my editor but kept waking up tossing and turning, thinking, *I have to change this, I need to adjust that*, etc. Internally I just felt I was missing something. I usually know when God is speaking to me because it's persistent and doesn't go away until I deal with it. So here is what I feel I am missing.

The last chapter might have been hard for some. As a Christian I can't add or take away from the Bible. God gives a drastic warning for anyone who does that. Read Revelation 22:18-19. I fear God more than I fear men or look for the applause of men and women. Our focus should be serving and looking for the approval of an audience of only one—God. No one need worry about or even give Hell a thought if you have made Jesus Lord and Savior of your life. We know Hell is real and that should instantly activate mercy in us for those that don't know God.

As I look back through my life, I am thankful God is who He says He is. God says, *"I am gentle"* (Matthew 11:29). God is patient (2 Peter 3:9); God is good (Psalm 107:1); God is love (1 John 4:16). Read Psalm 103:8. One of my favorites is (Exodus 34:6): *"A God merciful and gracious, slow to anger, and abounding in steadfast love and faithfulness."*

When I first heard the song, "Goodness of God," by Jen Johnson, I would well up with emotion as I listened to the words. They have been so true for my life. The tears would stream down my cheeks as I thought about God's love for me, His patience waiting on me as I was backslidden, living out my sinful will, His hands of protection in so many situations I got myself into, His abounding grace and mercy for me. God has been faithful and merciful to me.

We read in the Bible the story of the woman caught in the act of adultery (John 8:1-11), the story of God's love for the Woman at the Well divorced five times and now living with a man (John 4:1-42), and another powerful story of the Prodigal Son (Luke 15:11-32)—a boy that takes a portion of his inheritance and turns his back on his family, squanders the money caught up in sin, embarrasses his family, and disgraces his father. He eventually loses it all and comes to the end of himself knowing what he has done, has nowhere to go but back to his father. His father greets him ecstatic with open arms full of love, grace, and mercy. The boy in this parable represents you and me, the father represents Jesus.

As I shared earlier, I think one of the most important verses in the Bible is (John 3:16) but the next verse is just as important: (John 3:17): *"For God did not send His Son in the world to condemn it but to save it."*

We see the absolute love and mercy of God in all three stories *without* condemnation. God is merciful. The word "mercy" is referenced 276 times in the Bible from beginning to end (http://kingjamesbibledictionary.com). God is a God of love and mercy.

I remember watching the movie, *The Passion of Christ*, by Mel Gibson. I went through so many emotions watching that. I remember being angry with the chief priest for causing Jesus to be crucified. I was angry with the Romans for their part in having Jesus crucified. I was angry with the crowd when they cheered and called for Jesus to be crucified and to release Barabbas. But then it dawned on me. It was *my* sin that put Jesus on that Cross. They didn't take His life, He laid it down for you and for me.

(Romans 8:12): *"For I will be merciful to their unrighteousness, and their sins and their lawless deeds I will remember no more."*

(James 2:13): *"Mercy triumphs judgment."*

(Psalm 103:8): *"The Lord is merciful and gracious, slow to anger, and abounding in mercy."*

We all love the song, "Amazing Grace." It is sung at many funerals. The story behind that song is John Newton was an alcoholic, miserable, mean slave owner who surrendered his life to Christ when he was at sea and a horrific storm almost capsized the ship. In his hour of desperation, he cried out to God. God in His love and mercy answered that prayer, and with a shift of the ship filled the hole with cargo so the ship was able to drift to shore. God's mercy was now written in a song for you and me (http://swordofthespirit.net).

Everything in the Bible is there for our benefit. Look at the two thieves on the Cross. One denied Jesus and one simply believed. The one who believed had nothing to offer Jesus. He couldn't bow to Him in prayer, he wasn't baptized, confirmed, able to take Communion, and he didn't even say the sinner's prayer. All these things are great for our spiritual walk and draw us closer to God but it's for one reason and one reason only—believing Jesus is who He says He is, the Son of God. Jesus said, (Luke 23:43): *"Truly I tell you, today you will be with Me in Paradise."* Folks, this is the mercy and grace of God.

****

Let me give you some good news. Yes, the Gospel is the Good News— this beautiful, wonderful message of God's redemption of sinful humanity through the death and resurrection of His Son, Jesus Christ, but I want to share even better news. You are not a thief and you are not nailed to a cross dying in your last moments of life. You have time to make Jesus Lord and Savior of your life. One of my favorite videos is "The Cross" by Billy Graham. You can watch this on YouTube. Please take the time to watch this short video if you get a chance…powerful video! The Cross shows us God's overwhelming love but it is offensive to many because it does demand something of us.

Folks, most of this book is about God's amazing, relentless love for us. His gentleness and patience as he waits on us to choose Him over our own destructive ways. He will not violate our free will, He is always there with open, loving arms and His incredible grace and mercy for us. But we need to have a healthy fear of God, a reverence for Him, an awe of Him and who He is (Matthew 10:28). Do not be afraid of those who kill the body but cannot kill the soul. Rather, fear the one who can destroy both soul and body in Hell.

Think about it: some of you would be in awe of meeting your favorite rock star, celebrity, professional sports player, or even your favorite president. This is the God who created those famous people, created the moon, the stars, the galaxies, this entire earth which is His footstool. He holds your existence. We need a healthy fear of God (Isaiah 33:6). He will be the sure foundation for your times, a rich store of salvation and wisdom and knowledge; the FEAR of the Lord is the key to this treasure. I shared in an earlier chapter I have a few memories of my dad chasing us with a belt or we had to each wait in line to get our spanking. That was a healthy fear. I knew next time I acted out of line with the babysitter or my mom or dad, there were going to be consequences. Yes, my dad loved me, the Bible says discipline is love (Hebrews 12:5-9). My dad was disciplining me to protect me from making bad decisions that could harm my life and others. When you look at it in this context, it helps you to understand it better but also remember, God is perfect.

God hates sin because He knows what it does to His children. Do you think if our politicians and world leaders had a healthy fear and reverence for God, our country and this world would be in this mess? If they truly understood they will be standing before God giving an account for their actions, their leadership, maybe they'd be more careful with their decisions. I see some of these politicians and they are already past life expectancy which is mid-seventies in most parts of this country. It baffles me that these people do not think they are going to be held accountable before God. This is their eternity forever which they are nonchalant about. Just because they say "God bless America" when they're done does not mean they are in right standing before God. Look at their actions.

In Dr. Jeremiah's study Bible in the notes section at the bottom of page 1801 of 2 Peter, Chapter 2, it says, "Only a deeply committed, personal relationship with Jesus delivers people from divine judgment." You must love Jesus with your whole heart. Think of it this way. If someone tells you they love their wife or husband but they are flirting with every girl and boy out there, treating her or him with disrespect and even cheating on her or him, is that love? NO! That's not love. When you love someone, you respect them and try to please them to the best of your ability. No, we are not perfect, yes, we fall short and make mistakes.

Yes, the Cross demands something of us. Don't stress—I've felt what you're feeling right now. Listen to this next statement I make very carefully. "You cannot walk the Christian walk absent of God's Holy Spirit." When you invite Jesus into your heart He sends you the helper. I love what Jesus does when you invite Him in, He changes you and transforms you from the inside out. He gets rid of all that junk and baggage weighing you down. He guides and walks with you and helps you through. Yes, He is gentle, patient, and loving, but He knows this sin in your life is hurting you, separating you from Him.

God said David was a man after His own heart. King David committed adultery and was responsible for a man being murdered. How could God say a man like David was a man after His own heart? God loved David because David loved God, sought after Him, and tried to please God despite his failures. Some of those failures were big but most importantly David had a repentant heart. He knew he was wrong and God is Holy. Read Psalm 51, which David wrote in repentance to God. This psalm will move you. The Bible isn't a rule book, it's a loving letter to us. God knows we are human, He knows we are going to fall short…it's about the heart. Folks, the Bible says the fear of God is wisdom. A healthy fear and awe of God protects your walk with Him. The goodness of God draws us into repentance but the fear of God does too. Repentance is being sorry for your sin and turning from it. But repentance leads to God's forgiveness which is the mercy of God. Not only is it the mercy of God but it is cleansing to us and frees us of guilt and shame. It's freedom knowing we are forgiven and as far as the East is to the West, He remembers our sins no more (Luke 1:50). His mercy extends to those who fear Him, from generation to generation. Fear of God, repentance, and forgiveness is God's mercy for us. Does that mean that if you're on your deathbed and cry out to Jesus, He won't answer? No, I'm not saying that. (Romans 10:13): *"Everyone who calls on the name of the Lord will be saved."* You might not have a deathbed, for one, but don't you want to know if you die today you are spending eternity with God? Not only is this book about the beauty of walking with God, but getting to know

Him. This is a gift in itself, but you will spend eternity forever absent of pain, suffering, and engulfed in God's love and presence united with others who've also made Jesus Lord and Savior of their lives. Remember what the Holy Spirit spoke to me which I shared in Chapter Nineteen: *"Pray that Jason and Anna make Jesus Lord and Savior of their lives."* Another powerful short four-minute video is on YouTube by Francis Chan called "The rope illustration." Please take the time to watch this powerful video. It just shows you how we humans get fixated in this short existence called life and we take no time to plan or think about our eternity. This is my heart in writing this book that you will come to know this all-powerful, loving, Holy God while you are here but that you will spend eternity forever with Him too. One day when you stand before Him you will not get justice but mercy because of Jesus.

We will never have all the answers. On this side of eternity, the Bible says we see through a cloudy glass, a foggy mirror, but one day we will see Jesus face to face and we will then understand (1 Corinthians 13:12-13). One day as His love pierces you from His eyes and you are overwhelmed in His presence, you will be thankful for your faith in Him. The Bible says while we are here on this journey (Hebrews 4:16) let us come boldly to the throne of grace, that we may obtain mercy and find grace in our time of need.

Before the ride is over, let's ask God for His mercy for America. That is our only hope.

Chapter Thirty-Three

The Only Hope for America

My family and I were in Wildwood, New Jersey, for a short vacation on the Fourth of July 2021. I was sitting on the balcony where we were staying, overlooking the boardwalk and the ocean, watching people. They were showing their patronage to this country with what they were wearing and the groups of people walking together with our flag held high, then "The Star-Spangled Banner" started to play. I rose to my feet and put my hand over my heart and my eyes began to well up with emotion. I am so proud of this country and so thankful for those who shed their blood, and those who have sacrificed so greatly for our freedoms. Patriotism was ingrained in us. My father taught us to love and respect our country. He told us never to let the flag touch the ground, take your hat off, put your hand over your heart, stand with your head held high and your shoulders back as the National Anthem is being played. But I was also so full of emotion thinking how many don't appreciate this great country and are trying to tear it down.

We live in the greatest country on earth and ever created. This country was given in answer to prayer, through prayer, and formed from prayer. We have had the favor of God on this land. No other republic constitution has lasted this long. Most only survive twenty years, if I remember correctly. We are the envy of the world; everyone wants to live in the United States of America. Those that despise us are either evil or jealous. "We are the shining city on the hill," as President Ronald Reagan stated. We shine bright because of the favor of God on this land and all we do around the world for those in need. Our first President, George Washington, on Inauguration Day, got on his knees and dedicated this country to God in prayer.

A large majority of the 56 men who signed *The Declaration of Independence* were in some form of ministry to the Lord. Many of our Founding Fathers were deeply religious men of God and involved in their churches, some were founders and presidents of Bible societies. *The Declaration of Independence* refers to God and Creator. It also states, "We are endowed by our Creator, life, liberty, and the pursuit of happiness." And this is not to be infringed upon by our government. The Constitution includes the presence of God and states, "The Year of the Lord."

The sovereignty of God formed this country. After weeks of not coming into agreement at the Convention in 1787, Benjamin Franklin suggested they return to prayer, because prayer is what got them there. *How quickly we forget.* On June 28, 1787, Benjamin Franklin said, "In the beginning of the contest with Great Britain, when we were sensible of danger, we had daily prayer in this room for divine protection. Our prayers, Sir, were heard, and they were graciously answered. All of us who were engaged in the struggle must have observed frequent instances of superintending providence in our favor. I have lived, Sir, a long time, and the longer I live, the more convincing proofs I see of this truth—that God governs in the affairs of men. And a sparrow cannot fall to the ground without His notice, is it probable that an empire can rise without His aid?" (christianpost.com God and the Constitution)

Our schools used to include prayer as part of the school day, until a 1962 US Supreme Court decision banned school-sponsored prayer. This was the beginning of the demise of our country. There has been a slow fade up till recently of pushing God out of our country. We are now steamrolling and if we don't stop, America will be a memory and our great land will cease to exist.

With the recent pandemic crisis, we had many governors shut down the churches but leave liquor stores and abortion centers open. Our Christian leaders were "between a rock and a hard place" for many reasons: (1) If they opened they could be arrested or fined, which in my opinion is a violation of our Constitutional rights; (2) Because many of their congregants were living in fear, many were paralyzed by it. Many didn't know what to do, but let me share what we can start preaching and teaching now so if this ever happens again, we are ready.

(2 Timothy 1:7): *"For God hasn't given us a spirit of fear; but of power and of love, and of a sound mind."* Fear does not come from God. If it doesn't come from God, then we know who it comes from—Satan! God gives you the breath in your lungs, God allows your heart to beat. I love the song, "Great are You, Lord" by Casting Crowns, where the message is that we live because He allows it. Folks, if you're walking with God, death has no sting! (1 Corinthians 15:55): *"O death, where is thy sting? O grave, where is thy victory?"*

A few years ago, I had some medical issues. My bloodwork came back indicating my platelets were low, along with some other flags. My spleen was enlarged, and my doctor ordered a CAT-scan and found some nodules on my lungs and a small mass on my liver. I'll be honest,

I wasn't feeling that well and thought I was in some serious trouble. I remember thinking, *Lord, anything but lung cancer*, but rather than feed into fear I said, "Lord, my life is in Your hands, this is Your temple, and no matter what, You are with me. I would love to finish out some years with my wife, kids, and grandkids, but if You call me home, I'll be in Your presence."

(2 Corinthians 5:8): *"Absent from the body, present with the Lord."*

This is why I stress to my kids to make Jesus Lord of their lives. I love them too much and the thought of them not being in Heaven with me horrifies me. Not everyone goes to Heaven, like our politically correct society wants us to think. For every verse on Heaven, there are three on Hell. My relationship with Jesus will not get my children there. I like what I heard Ann Graham Lots say: "There are no grandchildren in Heaven," meaning we are all individually children of God responsible for our relationship with our Creator. That's the whole purpose of this book—to get you to know this amazing God and inherit salvation.

After many doctor visits, everything is okay. I do not want to negate that having a virus that can cause severe breathing problems in some is not scary. I am compassionate to this but I do not want fear to consume or cripple your healthy existence. Satan uses fear to control and torment you if you feed into it. I have battled anxiety and occasionally it tries to rear its ugly head so I understand its grip, but rather than feed into it I run to God and the tormentor flees. God uses *"Fear not"* throughout the Bible. Anytime you feel fear, run to God and He will help you deal with what issues reside in your heart and mind, through a process He will give you a peace beyond understanding that is a promise to those who love Him (Philippians 4:7). No one should be ignorant of their health. Use common sense and wash your hands, eat right, take vitamins, and leave the rest to God.

Churches in my opinion should stay open and those who open the door to Satan and let fear in will stay home, sadly. Churches please honor God and strengthen His people. I am thankful for all that Christian leaders do. I understand the Church was caught off guard but we now know in the future how to handle this if it ever happens again. I never want to criticize the Church, I appreciate what all those called are doing. COVID is now treatable and we have drugs that work with great success. When I was doing research I ran across some alarming statistics—that so many people in the ICU for health-related conditions are very low on Vitamin D3. We live in a time where we are not always being told the truth, and we don't know what to believe. That's why we need to pray for discernment. Your body is the Temple of the Lord, be careful what you inject into it.

****

Let's address another issue taking this country down: Racism.

Everything we hear nowadays is racist. What does racism do? It divides a country. Jesus states, (Mark 3:25): *"And if a house is divided against itself, that house cannot stand."* Racism stirs up anger, unforgiveness, and bitterness in the heart. It creates turmoil. I watch as people want to put a sticker on their car or a sign on their lawn, march in a parade, and think that constitutes they're not racist. Make sure whatever sticker you put on your car, whatever sign you put on your lawn, and with whomever you march, that you and they stand for love, unity, and peace; that they are for the nuclear family, love God, and never riot when they don't get their way or cause division. Martin Luther King, Jr. would never have been a part of tearing down cities, ruining businesses, and hurting people. Everything he did was inspired by the Bible, and that's why he was so successful. I love what he said, "Love is the only thing that can turn an enemy into a friend."

When I first drew close to God, I remember going before Him and asking if I had any racism in my heart. I felt the Lord was prompting me to read the book, *Uncle Tom's Cabin*. So I went to the library, checked it out, and read a few chapters. It was so depressing I had to put the book down because I couldn't read it anymore. I felt the Lord speaking to my heart, *"Jon, you're not racist but you lack compassion."* This opened my eyes to what these beautiful people had to go through, which was pure evil. We must be real before God and true to ourselves. We can put on a facade and tell people we're not racist or act like we're not racist, but the only person we fool is ourselves if we hide it in our hearts. Sometimes we need God to show us what is hidden in our hearts. I suggest that everyone do this, no matter your race or religion. This will protect you from one day standing before God and hearing, (Matthew 7:23): *"And then will I profess unto them, 'I never knew you: depart from Me, ye that work iniquity'."* This scares me to death.

Always remember to be honest with God, He knows the heart so you're not fooling anyone. I regularly ask God to examine my heart and correct what's wrong. This protects your walk with Him. I think what saddens me most is we have people who put Reverend in front of their name at these marches, yet all you see from them is division, you don't see them trying to heal the hurt, show love, or unite people as the Bible guides us to do.

(Matthew 5:9): *"Blessed are the peacemakers; for they shall be called the children of God."*

I would love to see another Martin Luther King, Jr. step up—*a true leader.* Chris Singleton comes to mind. His mother was killed at church during a Bible study, at the Charleston Church massacre. This young man represented Jesus Christ, and he was powerful! When I listened to him, I got choked up with emotion at such forgiveness and love. I was so moved by the picture of Christ he was bringing forth as he spoke. Only a genuine follower of Christ could do this. His mother had to be smiling down with the Lord from above, so proud of her boy! When you go through something gut-wrenching and painful, you must ask God to help heal your heart and bring forth genuine forgiveness. I have found that God will lead me to pray for that person and ask the Lord to see that person through His eyes, and help me forgive. I choose to forgive the man responsible for my brother's death. His actions of cutting corners and not securing the work area because of time and money caused my brother's tragic death. God doesn't ask us to forgive others, it's required (Matthew 6:15). It might happen quickly and it might take a little time, but what's most important is you have given the battle to God.

Some people have such deep hurts that only God can help them heal. He wants you to heal because God knows the damage of bitterness, unforgiveness, and resentment. I know some of you have such deep hurts that only God can help you through it, but remember, forgiveness is not an option. (Matthew 6:14-15): *"For if you forgive other people when they sin against you, your Heavenly Father will also forgive you. But if you do not forgive others their sins, your Father will not forgive your sins."*

God knows what unforgiveness does to you and everyone around you. When you forgive someone it's like setting a prisoner free, realizing the prisoner is *you*. It is said forgiveness and freedom go together. I also like the saying, "Bitterness only consumes the vessel which carries it." Bitterness only hurts *you*. Holding onto bitterness, unforgiveness, and resentment is toxic to you and can even cause illness and disease. Let's start praying God raises up more peacemakers to lead this cause, full of love with the gift of unity, so they can squash and put out this racist fire trying to ignite and divide this beautiful country. Don't fall for the trap of the evil behind this.

If you have a genuine heart for Jesus Christ, you shouldn't see skin color. I remember hearing Billy Graham preach on this. God had a black man, Simon, help carry Jesus' cross to his crucifixion when he was so weak from the beatings and torture. What an honor God gave to help carry the Cross and defeat sin and death once and for all. He gave that honor to a black man. Jesus asked John the Apostle to look after his mother as he hung from the Cross in His last moments. What an honor to entrust this responsibility to look after His earthly mother to someone he loved and cherished. This honor was given to a white man. Jesus wasn't black nor was he white. God showed us that He is not the black man's God and he is not the white man's God, He is *everyone's* God! I say to every black man and woman there are so many of us that are sorry for what your people have had to go through and we pray for God's comfort for the pain of these thoughts and memories to be completely healed. The Apostle Paul says, (Philippians 3:13): *"But one thing I do; forgetting those things which are behind, and reaching forth for what lies ahead."* I know these memories are awful and despicable but with the help of God put this ugly past behind you. Forgiveness has no past with God's overwhelming love. Let us bring this country forward with love and compassion, united in Christ!

****

Another area which concerns me is preachers at the pulpit saying that politics won't fix America. I agree, but the Christian needs to be involved with supporting those whose views align with the Bible, and it is a Christian's responsibility to vote. At this point in America, we are beyond politics. We are in a full-out spiritual war. Roughly sixty to sixty-five percent of the population identifies as Christian in America. If they all voted godly men and women into office, we wouldn't be in the mess we're in here in America. *We need to vote for the Bible* and always ask ourselves, "What would Jesus do?" Life is sacred to God and we must protect it.

(Jeremiah 1:5): *"Before I formed you in the womb I knew you, and before you were born I consecrated you."*

(Genesis 9:6): *"Whoever sheds the blood of man, by man shall his blood be shed, for God made man in His image."*

(Psalm 139:13-16): *"For You formed my inward parts; You knitted me together in my mother's womb. I praise You, for I am fearfully and wonderfully made."*

****

In the Old Testament if you hurt a pregnant woman you would be charged for two murders. Before I go any further, if you have had an abortion or are part of an abortion and repented of this, you are forgiven. God loves you. He has forgiven you and as far as the East is to the West, your sins are forgiven, He remembers them no more. You need to accept that forgiveness. I don't judge you and no one has the right to judge you. We all have fallen short of the glory of God (Romans 3:23). This is for both women and men. I know men who struggle with this guilt. Accept God's forgiveness. The good news is that with God you'll be reunited with that child one day in glory.

I do not intend to bring up wounds, but prevent future abortions. There are variables. If a woman is raped, incest, or the health of the mother, she shouldn't be forced into a decision beyond her control, but even in those rare and awful situations, I pray the woman would seek God for wisdom. God has a beautiful way of turning ashes into beauty. Some struggle with "my body, my choice," or that this is political. This is not political at all. This is Biblical. But if you are struggling with this, please take the time to watch the movie, *Unplanned*. This is based on the true story of a clinical director for Planned Parenthood who comes to know Jesus and her eyes are opened to what truly happens when an abortion takes place. The doctor in this movie, Dr. Anthony Levatino, used to perform abortions. God changes his heart and opens his eyes as well, and he is now sickened over what he has done and becomes an advocate for life. I pray if you struggle with this, God will open your eyes.

We must vote men and women with godly values into office. Don't just listen to their words, make sure actions back up their beliefs. (Proverbs 29:2): *"When the righteous thrive, the people rejoice; when the wicked rule, the people groan."* More importantly, we need to pray. Satan shudders when we pray. We need to pray not only for godly leaders, but also for our existing leaders in office. We need to pray for God's favor over this country. My dream for this country is that we honor God, that it would be politically correct to honor God. That the Church would unite in love together—Baptist, Lutheran, Methodist, Pentecostal, Catholic, let's come together as one front.

(Ecclesiastes 4:12): *"Though one may be overpowered, two can defend themselves. A cord of three strands is not quickly broken. We are one family of believers and united with God we are unstoppable."*

(Isaiah 54;17): *"No weapon formed against you will prosper."*

(Matthew 16;18-19): *"And I tell you, you are Peter, and on this rock I will build My church, and the gates of Hell shall not prevail against it. I will give you the keys of the Kingdom of Heaven, and whatever you bind on earth shall be bound in Heaven, and whatever you loose on earth shall be loosed in Heaven."*

Did you just hear that? The power we have as men and women of God, united in love and prayer—we are *unstoppable*!

The only hope for America is for us to turn back to God, to have a heart of repentance, to pray without ceasing, to unite as one front in Christ, and to honor God. Because the Church is not unified, we are like scattered soldiers on the battlefield. WE NEED TO UNITE. Unity, love, and repentance.

(2 Chronicles 7:14): *"If My people, who are called by My name, will humble themselves and pray and seek My face and turn from their wicked ways, then I will hear from Heaven, and I will forgive their sin and I will heal their land."*

We as Christians need to truly represent Jesus well. What does that look like? Love and humility, kindness, and living a life pleasing to the Lord. If we try and consistently show genuine love, humility, and kindness, the goodness of God will draw people into repentance (Romans 2:4). Repentance moves the heart of God, and my prayer is we will live to see the greatest revival and awakening, and this will save our shining city on a hill, and America the Beautiful will be preserved. My prayer is that all you mighty men and women of valor rise up, unite, and lead this country back to God to honor and glorify Him. It is said that for evil to persist, it is for good men and women to do nothing. Jesus said we are to occupy till He comes (Luke 19:11-13).

Billy Graham said, "Courage is contagious. When a brave man takes a stand, the spines of others often stiffen." Leaders unite! Faith can move mountains but more importantly a country to its knees in prayer. Come, my fellow believers, let's start ten million men and women marches for this country to honor our Holy, loving, faithful God, and only elect men and women of God. Jesus said, *"My house is a house of prayer."* We need to become a country of prayer. I pray just like Elisha prayed that God would open the eyes of his servant Gehazi, that our eyes would also be opened so you all know we are not alone. There are horses and chariots of fire all around us, angels with their swords drawn released through the prayers of God's people. Be encouraged, my friends, nothing is impossible with God. And I'll bet Jesus will stand up for us like he did Stephen, the first martyr, and cheer us on.

(Psalm 33:12): *"Blessed is the nation whose God is the Lord, the people He chose for His inheritance."*

With repentance, prayer, unity, and honoring God, we can return to a fresh outpouring of God's favor on this land.

Come, Holy Spirit, please come heal our country.

Closing Comments

How does God take someone who hardly read anything till his mid 30s, with zero interest in school, and place it on his heart to write a book? As I spent time with God, the desire to write came to me. I would start taking notes on my iPhone. I was encouraged by a Jewish customer whom I met through my lawn business who has authored many books. She gave me a very generous gift toward my first and only computer and helped me get started in my writing. I have such respect and gratitude for her and she will always hold a special place in my heart. But what started out as a vision, a dream, turned into a reality. I had to go on faith.

So many of us think that God walked alongside Noah, Joseph, Joshua, Mary, Elizabeth, John the Baptist, Peter, John, Paul, and many others in the Bible holding their hand, coddling them, but He did not. Just like you or me, He gave them a word or a prompting and they had to trust in the one whom they serve. Read Hebrews, Chapter 11, the faith chapter of the Bible. My prayer and my hope is that having read this book you will be inspired to have a personal relationship with Jesus Christ. Remember, it is *relationship*, not religion. God is alive and active in every detail of our lives. His Word is living.

Many people have a problem believing that God created the earth and the galaxies. For me it is hard to comprehend that there are seven billion people on this earth and God knows each one of us and every facet of our lives, every issue, big and small, that we struggle through. Not only does He know each of us intimately, He loves us all equally with a love beyond comprehension. When you draw near to Him and invite Jesus into your heart, He will make that clear on your journey.

One big paradigm shift I had was when I was reading a book, *The Seven Habits of Highly Effective People*, by Stephen R. Covey, that suggested the reader get quiet, somewhere without disturbances, and write their own eulogy. I did that and realized I was living backward, contrary to what I believed and wanted to be remembered for. As I wrote my eulogy I realized I wanted to first be recognized as a man of God. Second, I wanted to be remembered as a man who loved and was there wholeheartedly for his family, and third, I wanted to be recognized as a hard worker and a godly business owner. This woke me up to the fact that I had it backward. I had my business first, family second, and God last. I had to make a shift and put God first, family second, and work third. I did that, and guess what I got? I have a personal relationship with Jesus and am close enough and still enough to hear His voice.

In your hands is a book that was in the tapestry of my being on this journey called life, which is now part of *your* tapestry. Take the time to write your own eulogy. What does God have in store for you? What is your legacy going to be?

Two very important chapters of my experiences sum up and validate the Bible. I shared that God allowed me to see into the spiritual realm and showed me the pure evil we are up against. Demons do exist and there's a place they live called Hell. They have come to rob, torment, kill, and separate you from the love of God now and forever. They want to bring as many people as possible to Hell with them to share in their eternal doom. Also, my beautiful experience with Jason in the elevator and hearing the Holy Spirit speak clearly in my right ear (John 3:16). Yes, we are always to use the one and only Holy Bible to guide us, but please take these two powerful experiences of seeing and hearing to encourage you to open your heart to Him. The Bible is a miracle from God, His love letter and guide for this journey we call life. You are a soul on an earthly experience. There is a Heaven and there is a Hell. Only those who make Jesus Christ Lord and Savior of their lives go to Heaven.

This is not only about eternity but what you are missing by not opening your heart to God—the beauty of walking with Him, the peace, contentment of knowing He is with you always. Your life could be a complete mess but it doesn't matter if you have God. There's a peace in any storm if you walk with Him (Philippians 4:6). There is absolutely nothing you can do or have done that is unforgivable. The Bible says, "Come as you are." He loves you too much to keep you that way.

(James 4:14): *"Life is a breath, a mist, then we vanish from this earth."*

Our journey here at any moment can end without notice. We will all one day stand before God and be accountable for the lives we lived and face judgment, BUT NOT FOR THOSE IN CHRIST JESUS. I love the song from Third Day, "Trust in Jesus." One day we will all stand before God to be judged. What will we say? That we trust in Jesus.

(Romans 8:1): *"There is no condemnation for those in Christ Jesus."*

(James 2:13): *"Mercy triumphs judgment."*

(Philippians 2:10-11): *"One day every knee will bow, every tongue will confess that Jesus Christ is Lord."*

I will do it with honor and a grateful heart now, proud of my Lord and Savior Jesus. **The biggest mistake of my life was running from God and not learning from my mistake. Don't run from God, run** *to* **Him.** If I learned that years ago I would have saved myself a lot of heartache. I pray if you haven't opened your heart to God that you will. If you fell away from your walk with the Lord, I pray you reunite with Him. Those walking with God: go deeper, He has more for you. I always think of that verse in (2 Timothy 4:10): *"Demas has deserted me because he loves the things of this life and has gone to Thessalonica."* For two thousand years the Apostle Paul is in Heaven in God's presence and Demas chose this life over that. The Bible is God's perfect redemptive love for me and you. The parable of the Prodigal Son is a perfect description of a loving God never turning His back on us even when we have turned our back on Him. He's right there waiting with arms wide open and no condemnation but full of love and forgiveness.

Scientists have found that when the sperm meets the egg and life is started, there is an explosion. A miracle has just happened. YOU ARE A MIRACLE BY THE WORK OF HIS HANDS, the God that spoke the world into existence by His breath, who hung every star, the God who says the earth is His footstool. More importantly, He says you are written on the palm of His hand and you are loved by Him. God wants to have a relationship with you, a relationship that lasts for eternity, one day absent of pain, suffering, hurt, death, and tears, but also the beauty of getting to know Him here.

Take a seven-day or a thirty-day challenge and read your Bible, listen to Christian music, go to church, and most importantly, invite Jesus into your heart as Lord and Savior of your life. See how God meets you right where you are. You will soon find that greater is one day in His presence than a thousand elsewhere. We have an amazing, gentle, patient, faithful, powerful, loving, Holy God who wants your journey to collide with His. It is your free will choice to make that happen. Eternity forever with God is not a hope, IT IS A PROMISE.

I've heard it said that when your heart and will align with God's...MIRACLES HAPPEN!

My prayer, my hope, my dream is you will find the Cross (Jesus) because therein lies the promise, and that this book will be used in a powerful way to *Inspire You to the Cross*!

Acknowledgements

I wanted to first thank my mom and dad. My dad is no longer with us. My parents' love and support created a strong foundation for this journey we call life.

Dad, you ingrained in me so many of life's skills to navigate the journey: Respect and manners will go a long way; Your handshake is your bond; A man has to do what a man has to do to take care of his family.

Thank you to my mom for living out her love for God. I am grateful for her prayers and for speaking God's wisdom into my life at such a young age. I could not only hear your prayers over me but feel the power and God's presence in them. Your faith was caught, not taught.

Thank you to my three sisters. Sure, I wish our journey was not so chaotic and filled with more harmony, but we all have a love for each other and with faith in Jesus we will one day be reunited with Dad and Jimmy. Maybe our journey was this way so that many could come to Jesus Christ through an example of our trials and tribulations but seeing God's overwhelming love and faithfulness.

I want to thank Our Savior's Lutheran Church, the rock of my foundation. I studied the lives of so many at Our Savior's while growing up, and they were great examples of genuine Christians. I have many memories of the beginning of life's journey here and Our Savior's somehow always still feels like home.

Special thank you to Pastor Rex Keener of Grace Fellowship. Thank you for following God's vision and dream of starting Grace

Fellowship. This church is being used powerfully by God, the presence of God is always here, but most importantly, thank you for pouring your heart and soul into your sermons and using your God-given gift to preach. Your preaching is so inspiring, it helped bring out what was deep inside—my love for the Lord. For the long season I was under your leadership, you taught me so much on navigating life and getting to know our amazing Creator. You are truly anointed by God! I will forever be grateful!

Special thanks to Dr. Charles Stanley, Dr. David Jeremiah, and Pastor Carter Conlon. Your anointed and gifted preaching and all the resources you supply have helped me on this journey walking closer with God. I can't tell you how many times listening to each of you I have been under conviction, encouraged, and just wept as you were explaining everything I was going through.

Special thanks to my hero in faith, Dr. Billy Graham. I was always mesmerized by your anointing, love, and humility. From a little boy I would watch your crusades on TV or your interview with Larry King. What little kid does that? The Lord has used you personally in a couple of ways to encourage me, knowing the admiration I have for you. Thank you to your family as they continue your legacy of preaching Jesus with love. We have a world that desperately needs Him.

Thank you to the Billy Graham Training Center at The Cove. The Training Center is such a great place to shut off life and seek God with no distractions and be engulfed in His beauty with the majestic mountains, babbling brooks, and so many quiet places just to listen for His gentle whisper. The presence of God is felt from the time you enter the premises until you leave. I have many memories of His presence there. I look forward to trying to get back each year and be alone with God.

Special thanks to Mrs. Spada who was such an encouragement and helped push me to get this book started. Your generous gift toward this computer, getting me set up, and teaching me how to use it to write was a huge part of this book coming to fruition. As a writer and author yourself, I am thankful for your encouragement when I questioned whether the Lord chose the wrong person. I will always have the utmost respect for you and will cherish our many conversations and friendship. I pray God's favor and blessing over you and your family regularly.

Thank you to Kathy Finlan who has published her first book, *Recovering From Generational Dysfunction*. Thank you, Kathy, for helping me find Lisa Petrocelli for editing, and Tiara Brown to design the amazing cover for the book. You helped me through many roadblocks in this process!

Thank you to Pastor Steve and Bethel Full Gospel Church. God has brought our family here for a season. Your preaching is gifted and powerful, it is unique, and with a sense of humor that helps to soak the strong message in deeper. I love the way the worship and service are so sensitive to being led by the Holy Spirit with regular altar calls. There is power in altar calls. Something in my spirit says this is the final ingredient in what God has been preparing me for. I still do not know exactly what that is, but time will tell. I so enjoy being a part of this Holy Spirit filled church.

I finish with those who God has entrusted to me. That have been alongside me on a huge part of this journey and the whole process of this book. A special thank you to my beautiful wife Kim, our daughter Devyn, son JonMichael, daughter Jillian, and my granddaughters Camille, Mila, and grandson Grayson. I am so blessed to call you my family and I love you all more than life itself.

Author's Note

Thank you for taking the time to read *Inspired to the Cross*. As I have shared, all profits from this book will be given back to glorifying God through His church and missions. The first miracle was me writing this book. Those that truly know me realize that. The second miracle will be getting this book into the hands of His people. You can be a part of that miracle. If this book has blessed you in some way, I ask you to prayerfully consider purchasing a few copies and getting them into the hands of others who need the understanding of how much God loves them. Maybe some will be led to buy many books and drop them off at a local prison, retirement home, nursing home, or whoever or wherever God prompts them to go with it.

There are so many broken and hurting people who need to know God's amazing grace, mercy, and love for them. He is their hope in this world which has become increasingly dark. You, me, and the message of this book can represent the light and love of Jesus. Do not ever underestimate what a small act of kindness, generosity, and love can do. You might just get the book into the hands of the next Mother Terresa or the next Billy Graham. Our God is big! Dream big dreams, pray big prayers, and stand back and watch in AWE how the God of the impossible moves!

(Numbers 6:24-26) "The Lord bless you and keep you; The Lord make His face shine upon you, and be gracious to you; The Lord lift up His countenance upon you; and give you peace."

In Christ,

Jon Kennedy

References

The Bible

The Bible is the most important book for us to read. It is God's primary way of communicating with us and if you really want to grow in your faith, start by reading the Word of God. Always pray prior to reading it and ask God to give you understanding and speak to you. Even if you do not understand what you are reading you are honoring God and God sees that. New Christians should start out in the Gospels and stay in the New Testament till God guides you to the Old Testament. I prefer *The Jeremiah Study Bible.* The beginning of every book of the Bible has an introduction to what you are reading in that book. The bottom of every page has study notes that help explain in more detail what you just read. Throughout the Bible, Dr. Jeremiah has many Essentials of the Faith pages going into more depth and many reflection and takeaway points to help you digest more of God's Word. You can install Dr. Jeremiah Turning Point App on your phone for many more resources and listen to daily short sermons.

Allen, James: *As a Man Thinketh*

This book teaches us the power of our thoughts.

Chapman, Dr. Gary: *The Five Love Languages*

This is an amazing book. It sells more every year. Dr. Gary Chapman teaches you how you and those you love receive and give love. Dr. Chapman has authored many other books to help in relationships.

Comfort, Ray: *Scientific Facts in the Bible*

This book was excellent! It shows you how God and science work together. Ray Comfort shares so much here to open your eyes to how much is in the Bible for our benefit and knowledge.

Covey, Stephen R.: *The Seven Habits of Highly Effective People*

I learned a lot from this book, which also caused my "a ha" moment when I used Covey's suggestions (see Closing Comments

Eldredge, John: *Wild at Heart (Discovering The Secrets of a Man's Soul)*

This book taught me to spend time with loved ones. We never know what tomorrow holds.

Graham, Billy: Angels: *God's Secret Agents*

This book was inspirational and moving. We are not alone.

Jeremiah, Dr. David: *Jeremiah Study Bible*

1 Corinthians 7:10-11 *Institution of Marriage.*

2 Peter Ch. 3, *The Mercy Chapter*

Mandino, Og: *The Greatest Miracle in the World*

This book really opened my eyes in so many ways. It was so inspirational to me and helped me to stay thankful and realize we are so blessed. When I get to Heaven I will find Mr.Og Mandino and thank him. Amazing to think he almost ended his life because he was in such a pit from many bad choices, but God had big plans for him and for that I am thankful.

Mandino, Og: *The Greatest Salesman in the World*

Peale, Norman Vincent: *The Power of Positive Thinking, by*

This book was very significant in my walk. It gave me a better perspective on how to handle my problems and stop letting them ruin me. Staying positive is important to your journey.